Kazakhstan

The
Business Traveller's
Handbook

D1432043

Gorilla Guides
Travel handbooks for the business jungle

KAZAKHSTAN

First American edition published in 2010 by
INTERLINK TRAVEL
An imprint of Interlink Publishing Group, Inc.
46 Crosby Street
Northampton, Massachusetts 01060
www.interlinkbooks.com

First published in Britain in 2010 by Stacey International

ISBN: 978-1-56656-799-2

Series originator: Max Scott
Series editor: Christopher Ind
Assistant editor: Charles Powell
Design: Nimbus Design
Photography: © Yuriy Kurbatov
Cartography: Amber Sheers
Printed in the UAE

Every effort has been taken to ensure this Guide is accurate
and up-to-date. The reader is recommended, however, to
verify travel and visa arrangements before departure. The
publishers cannot accept any responsibility for loss, injury
or inconvenience, however caused.

Opposite: The traditional Kazakh dress is still worn to this
day, especially to mark formal events and ceremonies, forming
an important part of this young country's identity.

Kazakhstan

The Business Traveller's Handbook

Michael Fergus
& Vitaliy Krotov

The cable car to Koktobe Mountain, which rises 300 metres above Almaty, offers spectacular views of the city. (see page 175)

Seemingly endess flower meadows carpet great swathes of Kazakhstan's steppe country each spring.

Completed in 2003, Astana's Bayterek tower has become the undisputed symbol of the new capital. (see p. 136)

Bolshoi Almaty Lake is fed by the glaciers of the Tian Shan Mountains and is an ideal day trip from Almaty.

The KazMunaiGaz building in Astana is one of the city's most imposing structures.

The dramatic red sandstone Charyn Canyon near Almaty is 80 kilometres long and, in places, 300 metres deep. (see page 174)

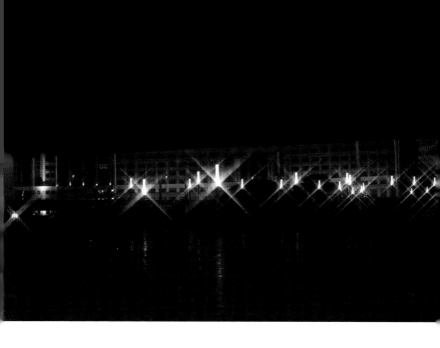

The Tian Shan mountains in winter offer excellent skiing. The Shimbulak Ski resort is easily accessible from Almaty. (see page 171)

The ministry of communication is housed in one of modern Astana's most distinctive towers, completed in 2005: now a landmark symbol of this city's newly acquired status as a key business destination.

Contents

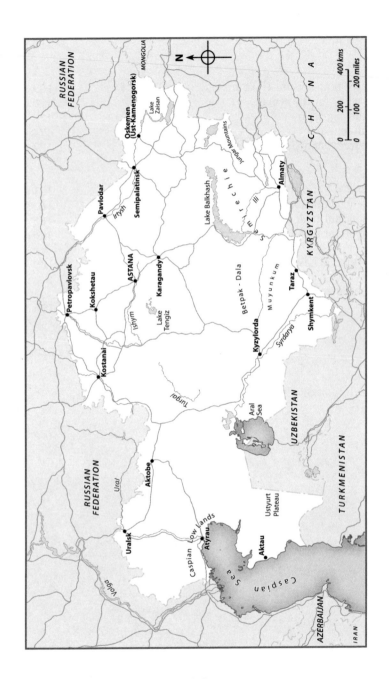

Kazakhstan

an overview
of the country

an overview
of the country

A bird's-eye view of the nation,
its history and the special features
that distinguish it from other countries
A condensed history
The modern country

1

Size matters

Most visitors to Kazakhstan can confirm the truth of this. It does not take long to realise that travelling in Kazakhstan is like traversing vast countries like Canada or Australia, and not at all like planning a week's business trip round several European countries. Of course this has a profound impact on how one does business in Kazakhstan.

For example: imagine a business trip from Almaty, the country's commercial capital in south-east Kazakhstan to Uralsk, the take-off point for the emerging Karachaganak gasfields, and the capital of West Kazakhstan province. The non-stop trip on an Air Astana Boeing 757-200 takes three hours 15 minutes. The distance – just over 2,000 kilometres – is the same as from London to Casablanca in Morocco. Uralsk is closer to Helsinki in Finland than it is to Almaty. By the time you get to Uralsk from Almaty, you are already two thirds of the way to Moscow. The same applies to the oil cities of Atyrau and Aktau on the Caspian Sea. Both are closer to Ankara in Turkey than they are to Astana and Almaty, Kazakhstan's most important cities. Thus it is not very practical to consider hiring a car and driving it. Visiting Kazakhstan's oil and gas centres by car would imply a trip of two or three weeks, and would not be practical in winter. The very size of Kazakhstan can often mean that a one-day meeting in a distant city can mean a three day trip including two days' travelling.

This example illustrates perhaps better than anything the importance of Kazakhstan's geography to doing business there. It is a big country straddling the divide between east and west. It most definitely has one foot in Europe, and one foot in Asia. Because it is so big Kazakhstan often feels like three countries in one. There is the 'European' one with the northern and western cities of Uralsk, Aktobe, Kostanay and Pavlodar. They have a distinct Russian almost 'Tsarist' feel about them. They are little different in size and character from their counterpart cities like Omsk and Chelyabinsk just over the border in Russia. Then there is a vast 'Eurasian' one made up of the steppe in central Kazakhstan, full of strategic minerals, wildlife, a few remaining nomadic horsemen and not much else – an ideal wilderness for launching and retrieving spacecraft, which is what the

1

Russians continue to do bang in the middle of the steppe at Baikonour Cosmodrome. Then there is the 'Asian' one, with the looming 6,000 metre high Tian Shan Mountains bordering China and Mongolia, the wonderful Islamic monuments of south Kazakhstan and the exotic Central Asian culture and peoples on the borders with Uzbekistan and Kyrgyzstan.

Although the roads are good, metalled and with little traffic, and the railways are stolid, reliable, if awfully slow, geography means that doing business in Kazakhstan necessarily takes a lot of time. Unless you are prepared to fly everywhere – and that is not always possible – you risk a lot of long car journeys through empty steppe lands merely to get from one centre to the other.

Population

Nor are you likely to see many folk on your way, because Kazakhstan is one of the least densely settled countries on earth. With 2.7 million square kilometres it is the largest landlocked country in the world, and the ninth largest overall – only a little smaller than India. But its population is a mere 15 million (a quarter of that of the United Kingdom). This means that there are a mere five persons per square kilometre in Kazakhstan whereas in the United Kingdom there are 248 in the same area. Karaganda Region, just one of Kazakhstan's 15 regions, is almost twice the size of the United Kingdom but contains fewer than 1.5 million people, most of whom live in the main city. It is not unusual to drive hundreds of kilometres in the Karaganda Region without seeing a soul.

A Tale of two cities

Until 15 years ago, geography was an even more important factor in doing business in Kazakhstan. Until around 1996 there was only one place to get to grips with business in Kazakhstan and that was in Alma-Ata, now known as Almaty. Everywhere else outside Alma-Ata was either a mining centre or fields of waving grain. There is no doubt that Almaty is and always was an Asian city, with its thronged markets, its ethnic mix of Kazakhs, Russians, Uighurs, Uzbeks, Tadzhiks, Mongols and many other races and its orchards of figs, almonds and pomegranates in the shadow of the snow-decked summits of the Tian Shan Mountains.

1

After the break-up of the Soviet Union and the emergence of Kazakhstan as a sovereign state in 1991 it soon became pretty evident to President Nursultan Nazarbayev and his advisers that it was not entirely practical to have a capital city lying over 1,000 kilometres from most of the country it presided over. In fact, Almaty is so far south and east in Kazakhstan it is closer to Islamabad in Pakistan than it is to many Kazakh cities. This worked well enough when the country was a subordinate republic of the USSR, where Alma-Ata served as a southern base for the Moscow-centred administration. But now, with nationhood thrust upon it, the problem was that Almaty was situated in the extreme south-east of a country about the size of Europe. It was like having Lisbon as the capital of Europe. For an independent sovereign government to function effectively it had to get closer to its own people – spread as they were so widely and so thinly over the steppes of Central Asia.

Capital city

In 1994 it was decided to transfer the capital of the newly independent country to a small provincial outpost at Akmola, 1,250 kilometres north and west of Almaty. This proposal was met at the time with much sneering and scepticism. Who on earth would move from the balmy, tree-lined avenues of Almaty to a small town in the freezing, windblown steppe? Yet a mere twelve years after the move, Astana has blossomed into one of the most exciting new capitals in the world.

It is either in Astana or in Almaty that you will land if you are doing business in Kazakhstan. It is these two cities upon which this book will concentrate because it is here that things in Kazakhstan happen.

In the beginning

Kazakhstan is one of the world's newest independent states, having declared its independence from the then Soviet Union on 16 December 1991. But, as much of today's Kazakhstan is featureless grasslands, steppe or desert, it has never been easy to fix firm borders or to define territorial boundaries. Its original inhabitants, nomadic herdsmen, were hardly the sort of people to let themselves be confined to national boundaries. It is

1

therefore only relatively recently that a nation state with firm and internationally recognised frontiers has emerged. The Kazakhstan entity as we know it today – stretching over 2,000 kilometres from the River Volga and the Caspian Sea in the west to the Altai and Tian Shan Mountains in the east – is probably the end result of the expansion of the Russian empire eastwards in the 19th century, and its various encounters with the local Kazakh population of the Central Asian steppes. This gradually helped to forge most of what are Kazakhstan's international borders today with Russia, China, Mongolia, Kyrgyzstan, Uzbekistan and Turkmenistan. There are traces of human activity from over 4,000 years ago in what is now Kazakhstan.

First known inhabitants

The Scythians (also known as the 'Saka') were legendary horsemen and metalworkers, who lived between 1,000 and 300 years before Christ. They were among the first known inhabitants of what is now Kazakhstan. Archaeological evidence shows that they developed a thriving culture in the remote and empty Altai Mountains on Kazakhstan's eastern borders with China, and that they spilled over into the steppes of Central Asia. The Scythians were masters in working with gold and other precious metals and developed a standard of gold-working which has never been surpassed elsewhere.

Archaelogical findings

The astonishing golden treasures of the Scythians can be viewed in Kazakhstan's National Museums in Astana and Almaty and are regularly lent to leading museums all over the world. Best known of these is the 'Golden Man of Issyk' which is essentially a cloak consisting of 4,000 gold platelets, discovered in a Scythian 'kurgan' or grave mound in south-east Kazakhstan in 1969. This has been dated to the sixth century BC by German archaeologists. More recently a series of discoveries have been made of mummified chieftains, perfectly preserved in the permafrost of the Altai Mountains. So perfectly preserved, in fact, that even their elaborate tattoos remained intact, as fresh as when they were made over 2,500 years ago, and accompanied by stunning golden jewellery.

Well over two thirds of Kazakhstan is trackless steppe and desert with varying sources of fresh water and grazing. Such country was not at all conducive to permanent human settlement and as such was inhabited by an endless succession of nomadic peoples. These were constantly on the move in search of seasonal water or pasture for their herds. They left no written records, and very few traces of material culture apart from graves. After 1,000 years stories and legends handed down by oral tradition tend to disappear. It is not until the coming of the Kazakh people about 600 years ago that we can begin to trace the emergence of something akin to a Kazakh nation and people.

The Coming of the Kazakhs

Martha Brill Olcott, one of the foremost Western authorities on Kazakh history, thinks that the Kazakh nation originated in the mid fifteenth century when Mongol pioneers settled in the rich pasturelands around present-day Almaty. Other groups quickly spread southwards to form the Uzbek and Kyrgyz nations. Ethnically the Kazakhs are thus close to today's Mongolians, although their language, like Uzbek and Kyrgyz, is a Turkic one, closely related to modern Turkish. All Central Asians are Sunni Muslim, although most visitors to Kazakhstan may see adherence to Islam as skin-deep. Of course there were Kazakhs before the birth of a Kazakh nation, and Kazakh culture in the form of poetry, music, philosophy and storytelling has existed for more than a thousand years.

Ethnic origin

Traditionally the Kazakhs have been divided into three Hordes (or extended clans), that is: the Great Horde, the Middle Horde and the Little Horde. These seem to have been based on the three main geographical areas in the Kazakh steppe suited for herding. The Great Horde was concentrated on southern Kazakhstan around today's Almaty. The Middle Horde inhabited central Kazakhstan and the Little Horde inhabited western Kazakhstan. Today's Kazakhs can still identify with their Horde.

The three Hordes

The Kazakhs, like their Mongol predecessors, were thus always nomadic herders, dependent for their livelihood on an intimate knowledge and exploitation of the arid steppes and deserts of Central Asia. This is a highly evolved socio-economy. The extreme continental climate with harsh, cold winters of high winds and snow and

1

hot, humid summers made it essential that the nomads and their herds of sheep, goats, cattle, camels and horses adapted to this demanding environment. They were extremely vulnerable to drought and snowstorms, and, if they lost their animals, faced starvation. To make the best of this hostile environment Kazakh nomads would develop wintering quarters in a sheltered area with a reliable supply of water where they might stay for up to four months.

Nomadic lifestyle

As spring came and the snows melted they would slowly move to their summer quarters, where a plentiful supply of water and grass was a prerequisite, where they might stay for three to four months. This lifestyle was perfectly adapted to the environmental conditions of the steppe. Tragically it was more or less totally eradicated by the Soviet collectivisation of agriculture in the 1920s and 1930s. Yet today's Kazakhs, whether urban bureaucrats or rural farmers, maintain a nostalgic link with their nomadic history. To be a nomad conferred great status.

All of Kazakhstan's legendary heroes, philosophers, musicians and soldiers were nomads. Korkhut Ata was a legendary eighth century musician and poet who invented the national musical instrument, the *kobyz*. Ahmed Yasawi was a twelfth-century poet-philosopher whose mausoleum in Turkestan near Shymkent rivals the better-known ones in Samarkand and Bukhara, and is one of Islam's architectural triumphs. Ablai Khan was the great eighteenth century Kazakh commander and military strategist. All of them were Kazakh nomads. In fact, with the growth of Kazakhstan's national consciousness and identity after independence there has been a noticeable resurgence in interest in Kazakh nomadic culture. Statues and giant portraits of Kazakh heroes are to be seen throughout the country.

One of the most stirring accounts of Kazakhstan's exotic history is to be found in *The Nomads,* a trilogy of novels written originally in Kazakh and Russian by Ilyas Yessenberlin (1915-83) and translated into English in 2000. It is a dramatised epic history of the Kazakh nation's struggle for identity in the four hundred years from 1500 to 1900. It is available in most bookshops in Kazakhstan.

Kazakhstan's culture, its language, its literature, its music, its poetry, its dress and its cuisine are a result of its nomadic origins and history. Seventy years of Soviet occupation sought to submerge this, but the visitor does not have to be in the country long to see signs of it. The national flag, straining in the wind on every public building in Astana, portrays the sun on a light blue background symbolising the sky on the steppe, with a golden eagle used by Kazakhs in hunting. The Kazakh language, with official encouragement, together with English, is making deep inroads in official business, displacing Russian. In winter Kazakhstan reverts to its nomadic roots as everyone wraps themselves in great fur coats and hats, often looking like extras from a Central Asian action film. National dishes are based on lamb, yoghurt and cereal, prime products of Kazakhstan's grazing lands. Music and dance ensembles are reviving the extraordinarily beautiful and elaborate traditional Kazakh costumes and instruments. Get outside the towns and into the steppe and you will soon see traces of Kazakhstan's nomadic history: the herdsmen on horseback, the yurts and the ornate Kazakh graveyards dating back many centuries.

Kazakh culture

The first major threat to the Kazakh nation came from the east, in the form of attempted invasions by the Dzjunghar people, predecessors of the present-day Uighurs from east Turkestan in what is now western China. They made continuous incursions into eastern and southern Kazakhstan before finally being repulsed. It was during these invasions that the Kazakh Hordes made their first overtures to the Russians for assistance – a forerunner to the coming of the Russians.

The Russians arrive

It was only in 1997 that the Kazakh people became a majority in their own country. Until then, for a very long time, there had been more Russians in Kazakhstan than Kazakhs themselves. The relationship between the Kazakhs and the Russians goes back over 500 years, and it is hardly surprising that it has had its ups and downs. On the one hand, the Kazakhs always viewed the Russians as potential allies and supporters in their struggles with Mongols and Djunghars in the east.

1

On the other hand, the Kazakhs were wary – with very good reason – of the Russians' ambitions to extend their power and their presence southwards and eastwards.

First contact with Russia

The Little Horde in western Kazakhstan was less than 1,500 kilometres from Moscow itself. It was therefore inevitable that they were the first Central Asian people that the emerging Russian state encountered as it expanded eastwards in the sixteenth and seventeenth centuries. The Russians' primary interest was in expanding trade to the east and they had two choices in this expansion: through negotiation and diplomacy or through military conquest. In their dealings with the Kazakhs they employed both methods. Often they did so in combination. The Russians, with their superior organisational, military and financial power, were perhaps bound to come out on top in the end against shifting alliances of nomadic herders. But on many occasions, the Kazakhs did give them a good run for their money. One of the most memorable of these occasions was the so-called 'Pugachev uprising' in 1773-4 where, together with Kazakh allies, a Cossack leader, Yemelyan Pugachev, captured the Russian city of Orel (now Uralsk, the capital of west Kazakhstan). The uprising was short-lived. Ablai Khan (1711-81), however, whom the visitor to Kazakhstan will see commemorated in stamps, in portraits, in statues and in designs throughout the country, was a more lasting obstacle to Russian dominance over the steppes in the eighteenth century. As the khan of the Middle Horde he was the consummate Kazakh politician and played the Russians and the Chinese against each other very skilfully. Much as his successors in modern times have been obliged to do. He is still regarded as one of Kazakhstan's greatest leaders and he was buried with honours at the magnificent mausoleum of Khoja Ahmed Yasawi in Turkestan (see above). Ablai Khan showed that only by balancing the interests and powers of Russia and China can Kazakhstan hope to safeguard and maintain its national identity. Another Kazakh *batyr* or warrior leader was Kenesary Kasymov (also commemorated by street names and statues in Astana) who led an unsuccessful ten-year (1837-1847) revolt against the Russian colonisers. Kenesary Kasymov was a direct descendant of Ablai Khan.

Implacably, however, Russian influence increased and expanded over the Kazakh steppes. This was achieved in many ways, through the infiltration of merchants bringing with them the Russian language and culture, through the building of military forts at strategic locations and with the introduction of the railways. Kazalinsk in Kyzyl orda Oblast, for example, was established by the Russians in 1867 close to the Aral Sea. Akmola (subsequently to become Astana) was established in 1830 and Fort Verniy (subsequently to become Almaty) was established in the foothills of the Tian Shan Mountains in 1854. The parallels with the 'taming' of the Wild West in the United States, which was proceeding at the same time, are striking.

Increase of Russian influence

Even more effective in securing Russian penetration of Central Asia in general and Kazakhstan in particular was the construction of the railways. Three were built in the latter half of the nineteenth century and the beginning of the twentieth century. There was the Trans-Caspian Railway, linking Krasnovodsk on the Caspian Sea with Tashkent in Uzbekistan, which took almost 30 years to build and was completed in 1906. There was the Trans-Aral Railway (also completed in 1906), which connected Orenburg in Russia to Tashkent. This opened up the whole of western and southern Kazakhstan to penetration from Russia. It linked at Arys through to the Turk-Sib Railway, which linked southern Kazakhstan with Siberia. The Turk-Sib Railway, which was completed in 1931, links Taraz in southern Kazakhstan with Barnaul far to the north in Siberia. All three railways continue to serve the commerce and populations of Russia and Central Asia and as communications links are as vital today as they were when they were built many decades ago.

Construction of railways

As in North America, the merchants, the forts and the railroads were a precedent to colonisation. The abolition of serfdom in Russia in 1861 generated a land hunger amongst the landless peasantry which could only be appeased by moving eastwards. The colonists were led by the Cossacks and were soon joined by a jumble of poor farmers, ex-convicts and religious exiles. By the end of the nineteenth century Kazakhstan had effectively been colonised and the native peoples, like the Amerindians, largely subjugated and pacified,

Land hunger and Russian settlers

1

although, like their counterparts in America, the Russian colonists never had an easy ride.

KSSR – the Kazakhstan Soviet Socialist Republic 1936 to 1991

There is no doubt that a proud, free and independent nation, as the Kazakh people had been, deeply resented the intrusion of Tsarist settlers. This resentment found its primary expression in disputes over land and water rights. By 1905 the Kazakhs had formed a nationalist party the Alash Orda which sought to articulate the grievances of the Kazakh people. At first the Russian revolution of 1917 gave the Kazakh people what they thought was an ideal means for expressing their discontent. It had become increasingly obvious that traditional, nomadic pastoralism as practised on the **Alash Orda** steppes was no longer sustainable, and a different **nationlist party** approach and a different, radical form of government were needed. However the heavy-handed methods of the Bolshevik revolutionaries led to a Civil War on the steppes with the ultimate defeat of the Alash Orda and the Kazakh parties. By 1920 the Bolsheviks could introduce a new economic policy based on a Soviet **Collectivisation** bureaucracy. Collectivisation of agriculture and the pastoral economy was introduced by Stalin, giving rise during the 1920s and the 1930s to great hardship and widespread starvation. Between 1920 and 1936 Kazakhstan was part of the Russian Federation but in 1936 became an autonomous Soviet socialist republic within the USSR.

Strangely enough, perhaps the most significant legacy of Soviet Kazakhstan for today's businessmen may not be the cities, the mines nor the industry of that sixty-year period. Instead it may prove to be the so-called 'Virgin Lands' policy of Khrushchev, whereby an area of 350,000 km^2 (an area about the size of Germany) in **Virgin lands** northern Kazakhstan and southern Siberia was put under the plough to produce cereals. After the death of Stalin in 1953, the Soviet Union faced a crisis of confidence and a food crisis. Seeking credit for acting quickly, Nikita Khrushchev organised the opening up of the 'Virgin Lands' between 1955 and 1965. Millions of 'pioneers' from Russia, Ukraine and Germany were brought in, and remained to settle in northern Kazakhstan. Several *oblasts* or regions in northern Kazakhstan still have a majority of non-ethnic Kazakhs 18 years after independence; a leftover from the Virgin Lands period. With the collapse of the Soviet Union and collective agriculture, much of the Virgin Lands were abandoned to their fate in the 1990s and still stand derelict. The contrast with the situation across the border in China is striking and, sometimes, chilling. In a world of land shortages and growing food shortages, the Virgin Lands of northern Kazakhstan represent a huge resource which could be as important as better-known oil, gas and mineral riches of the country.

During the Soviet era, Kazakhstan proved to be an economic powerhouse. It was a major coal, oil and gas producer, an exporter of ferrous and non-ferrous minerals and the most important source of agricultural cereals. In addition it had a relatively small, thinly-spread population so that polluting industry, weapons production and testing and the launching of spacecraft could safely be hidden away in the vast empty (and often forbidden) open spaces of Kazakhstan. The atomic testing base at Semipalatinsk where atomic weapons were tested in the atmosphere and underground (with devastating effects) between 1949 and 1989, is the best known of these.

Natural resources

Atomic weapons testing

But things could not last. Although Kazakhstan was a compliant and obedient republic, producing solid mineral, industrial and agricultural surpluses, even it could not avoid being touched by the glasnost and perestroika movements being hatched out in Moscow. In 1996 students protested against the replacement of Dinmuhammed Kunaev, ethnic Kazakh, as First Secretary of the Communist Party, by a non Kazakh, Gennady Kolbin. This was a sign of things to come. When the Soviet Union rapidly began to unravel in 1991, First Secretary Nursultan Nazarbayev was there to be elected President as the new Republic declared independence on 16 December 1991.

Election of Nursultan Nazarbayev

1

Today's Kazakhstan

Despite its fiercely independent history, after 70 years of
Soviet (and Russian) rule, Kazakhstan on independence
in 1991 had become thoroughly Russified. The Kazakhs
were a minority in their own country. Just over 40% of
the national population were ethnic Kazakhs (the rest
being Russian, Ukrainian, German, Greek and several
smaller minorities) and much of the Kazakh population
spoke only Russian and not Kazakh. In many ways
Kazakhstan, at the time, had been reluctant to take
on nationhood, having had it thrust upon it by events
outside its control, that is, the rapid dissolution of the
Soviet Union. In the early years of independence there
were fears of inter-ethnic clashes, of a mass exodus of
non-Kazakhs, of bankruptcy. In fact none of these
materialised. Quite the opposite.

Looking at Kazakhstan today, things clearly turned
out very differently. The idea of subordination to the
Russians, or to any other nation for that matter, is now
unthinkable. Although many relics of Soviet Kazakhstan
are still in evidence, the abandoned collective farms, the
bankrupt State industries and the derelict housing estates,
the business visitor will see for himself that Kazakhstan
has come a very long way in the past 18 years. To all
intents and purposes, in 1991 Kazakhstan was Russia.
Today it is an independent Central Asian nation with
excellent relations with Russia, Turkey, the United States,
China, the United Kingdom, India and Saudi Arabia.

Soviet economy

How did this come about? The country has been able to
throw off the Soviet legacy and to re-assert, slowly but
surely, the Kazakh/Turkic identity which it lost more
than a hundred years ago. But it has been an arduous
process. In 1991 Kazakhstan's economy was almost
inextricably bound up with the 15 other republics of the
Soviet Union. The central planning ministry in Moscow
sited industries in the various republics for strategic
reasons. For example, railway wagons for much of the
Soviet Union were built in a vast plant at Kazalinsk on
the steppes of Kyzylorda Region. The orders came in
with great regularity and the wagons were often
dispatched to the far corners of the Soviet Union, to
Murmansk on the Arctic Ocean or to Vladivostok on
the Pacific. This kept 5,000 people in work in remote

Kazalinsk. But when Kazakhstan gained independence, Murmansk, Vladivostok and the markets for Kazalinsk's railway wagons were suddenly in a foreign country, behind impenetrable toll barriers. The inevitable happened. Markets disappeared overnight. Kazalinsk could no longer import vital parts for its wagons. A plant, which a whole region depended on, slowly melted away. It also worked the other way around in Kazakhstan. Furniture factories in Almaty producing beds, chairs and tables in wood were suddenly cut off from their main sources of supply of timber, that is, republics like Estonia and Latvia. These newly independent countries found it impossible to export to the newly independent Kazakhstan. Nor was there any system of business credit between independent nations. There are hundreds of examples like this all over Kazakhstan where Soviet industry slowly withered away leaving thousands jobless. In many cases the industries had been imported to Kazakhstan from other parts of the Soviet Union, often along with the workers. When the industries failed, the workers from Belarus, Ukraine, Russia and the Baltics upped sticks and simply went home. This accounts for the fall in Kazakhstan's population in the first ten years of independence when many left the country for good. Much the same happened to Kazakhstan's collective agriculture, and all over the country you can see the derelict ruins of collective farms.

Loss of market after independence

And yet, since the beginning of the new millennium, Kazakhstan has registered record economic growth, with rates of up to 10% per annum. Kazakhstan has had to reduce rapidly its dependence on a classical Soviet command economy and switch to a market economy with an emphasis on individual rather than collective responsibility.

Record economic growth

How has it achieved these growth rates while large chunks of its traditional Soviet industry and agriculture have simply disappeared? Much can be attributed to political stability.

While the four other Central Asian republics of Kyrgyzstan, Tajikistan, Turkmenistan and Uzbekistan have experienced varying degrees of political turmoil

1

since independence, Kazakhstan can be seen as an oasis of calm in the borderlands between Russia, China and the Indian subcontinent. To such an extent that the Organisation for Security and Cooperation in Europe (OSCE), has entrusted Kazakhstan with its chairmanship in 2010 – the first country outside Europe proper to be entrusted with this position. The OSCE, which now has 56 members, works to promote stability, prosperity and democracy, mainly in Europe and Asia.

Political stability

There is no doubt that political stability in Kazakhstan has put it well ahead of its four Central Asian neighbours in terms of stability, prosperity and democracy. Political stability means that government and the bureaucracy could get on with essential work of fiscal reform, agricultural and industrial reconstruction, land reform and all the other things that were needed to convert this huge country from a remote and subservient Soviet republic to a bustling, self-confident, independent nation on excellent terms with the Islamic world, with its next-door neighbours in China and Russia, and with western Europe and America. Kazakhstan's political stability, of course, has not been without its critics and human rights organisations have kept the country under constant surveillance.

Almaty

The first-time visitor to Kazakhstan will usually arrive in Almaty or in Astana, and usually in the middle of the night (because of the four-five hour time difference between western Europe and Kazakhstan). When he awakens next morning he is in for his first surprise. In Almaty he will be astounded to find that he has somehow landed in the middle of the Himalayas. For there, right outside his hotel window tower the vast, snow-clad Tian Shan Mountains which rise to 5,000 metres (higher than the Swiss Alps) from the outer suburbs of the city. It is an experience even the seasoned traveller is not prepared for.

Astana

In Astana the experience is different, but perhaps no less striking. Here it is man-made, rather than natural, structures which jolt the complacent business visitor out of his reverie. Imagine glancing up from your scrambled eggs to see the newly completed Khan Shatyry Entertainment Centre, a gigantic polymer tent designed by Sir Norman Foster and Partners shimmering in the

morning light of the wintry steppe! And this is only
one of a succession of striking new buildings emerging
on the Astana skyline.

The Language issue

Despite the apparent sophistication of its two principal
cities, the legacy of the Soviet period is still very
important for some aspects of business life in the
country. Perhaps the most striking of these is the
continued predominance of the Russian language in
Kazakhstan. It is not the presence of the Russian
language that the visitor will notice almost immediately,
but rather the absence of English speakers, or speakers
of other western languages like French and German.
It is not unknown for a travel agency selling air tickets
not to have an English speaker at its sales desk.

Rarity of English speakers

It is difficult to imagine now, how isolated a Soviet
republic like Kazakhstan actually was only just over 20
years ago. Firstly you had to get yourself a Soviet visa –
not very easy at the best of times. Then, if you actually
wanted to visit Almaty or anywhere else in Kazakhstan
you had to negotiate with the authorities in Moscow
(usually Intourist) for permission to visit that particular
city (and specify the dates and specific accommodation
for your visit). Once you had managed that, you had to
negotiate with Aeroflot to fly there. While now you can
fly direct to Astana, Almaty and other Kazakh cities
from any number of cities in the West and in China on
Lufthansa, British Airways, Austrian, Turkish and Chinese
airlines, in 1985 there was only one way in, and that
was on Aeroflot from Moscow or some other Russian
provincial city. It is therefore hardly surprising that the
number of foreign visitors who actually managed to
make it to Kazakhstan before 1990 was miniuscule.

Isolation of Kazakhstan in the Soviet era

This almost total lack of foreign contact goes far to
explain why Kazakhstan feels remoter than it actually
is, and why the language problem in the Russian capital,
Moscow is much less than it is in Astana or Almaty. This
is because Moscow always had much closer contacts
with the outside world. Of course the situation, as is
the case all over the world, is changing rapidly. Young
people are motivated to learn English (and other western

Rise of English among young people

languages) as quickly as possible so as to have access to the Internet and to western business and culture generally.

In other words the language issue is a very real one for business visitors. That said, it has been solved in various ways. Some foreign businessmen (probably not a lot) know Russian or even learn to speak it. Most business folk, however, are thrown back on the services of interpreters and translators. This is not an ideal situation, but years of experience have made it a much less painful business than it was in the beginning. Now, however, more and more visiting businessmen are finding that their counterparts can in fact communicate easily in English. These are mainly younger folk who have studied English at school and had it topped up at college or on their studies overseas. English language documents no longer have to be translated laboriously into Russian. Simultaneous interpreters no longer have to be hired. It has been a long and slow process but things are improving quickly now.

Where there continues to be a problem for the businessman is in his contact with daily life. Most hotel staff and maybe even taxi drivers have an acquaintance with English. But you cannot expect this of shop assistants, train staff or policemen. There you still have to depend on sign language and goodwill in most parts of Kazakhstan.

Government efforts to promote Kazakh language

A poll held in November 2008 showed that only 36% of Kazakhstan's population speak fluent Kazakh whilst 90% claimed fluency or sufficiency in Russian, and 16% of the population speak no Kazakh at all. As a simplification it can be said that most of south and western Kazakhstan (closer to the other Central Asian republics) speak Kazakh, whilst the north and east of the country (closer to Russia) speak Russian. But there is no doubt about the government's determination to promote the use of Kazakh as the funds devoted to this task have increased from US$1 million in 2005 to US$42 million in 2008.

1

Security

Foreign visitors will often find that Kazakhstan, with its
Soviet background, has a noticeable respect for discipline
and public security. More so than in the wilder reaches
of the new Eastern Europe. This can mean less liberty,
but more security. As in the old Soviet days you are
supposed to register with the authorities when you arrive
in a new town, although in practice your hotel or your
host will do this. However, the police and public officials
have often been trained to show a healthy interest in the
welfare of foreign visitors. This can mean you are asked
by the police to identify yourself. As long as you have
your passport (which you are required to have on you
at all times) you will be fine. Similarly, you are often
asked to identify yourself in situations where this would
not be the case at home, for example, when buying a
railway ticket. On the other hand, if these seem minor
annoyances, it pays off in terms of public security. The
police and the authorities are often more vigilant than in
other countries, and should you be so unlucky as to get
into difficulties, the authorities are likely to be on hand
much more quickly than elsewhere.

2

investigating the
potential market

investigating the potential market

An outline of some of the myriad
organisations which exist to assist
the exporter, along with an
assessment of their focus and
likely relevance

Before arrival

2

Most international businessmen have a nodding acquaintance with many overseas markets. Most of us know something of other European countries, the States, the Middle East, South East Asia and even Africa. Through culture or tradition or through the Commonwealth, these areas have been part of Western consciousness for centuries. Which one of us does not know of a tobacco farmer in Zimbabwe, or had an uncle who worked on an oil rig off Saudi or a friend who exported biscuits to California?

But Kazakhstan . . .? Did any one of us know someone who was involved there? Hardly! The Iron Curtain ensured that none of us knew anything of Kazakhstan until less than 20 years ago. Not even its existence. Before that, it simply did not exist for the vast majority of us in the West. And if it did, the few who had heard of it knew it was a place where they tested atomic bombs in the atmosphere. A place one did well to steer clear of. A place no one would dream of visiting, far less do business in.

Unknown market

Thus countries as diverse as Malaysia and Mexico, South Africa and Singapore have a head start on Kazakhstan. Perhaps those who consider doing business in Kazakhstan and invest in this book are more adventurous, imaginative souls? Who knows?

So it is only in the past twenty years or so that a relatively few UN consultants, oil executives, bankers and financiers have started exploring this new, promising, but very little-known market. They got on the Lufthansa flight in Frankfurt in the early evening and landed seven hours later in the middle of the night in the middle of God knows where!

So it is smart to do some homework before you set off for Kazakhstan. Even if you have been there before. Because of its great size, Kazakhstan is quite diverse. If you have been to Almaty or Astana before, it does not mean that you know how things are in the Caspian region, 2,000 kilometres away to the west.

Research

Since most of the source material on Kazakhstan is in Russian (and possibly Kazakh) most western

2

businessmen will have to glean their knowledge at second hand from second-hand sources. Because Kazakhstan is very different from most other markets you are likely to be used to, it is very important that you prepare yourself very thoroughly before setting off. This chapter sets out the most reliable sources of information on your intended market.

Kazakhstan Embassies

Perhaps the best place to start on getting up to speed on Kazakhstan is the official one, that is, with the Kazakh Embassy. Kazakhstan has now established at least 50 embassies and missions throughout the world, including in the United Kingdom, the United States, Austria, France, Germany, Italy, Poland and Spain. Most of them have their own web pages. The Kazakhstan Embassy in the UK allows you to download a visa application form from its website:(http://www.kazembassy.org.uk). The website contains information on trade and investment, links to Kazakh institutions and general information on Kazakhstan. The Kazakhstan Embassy is situated at"

33 Thurloe Square
London SW7 2SD
Tel: +44 (0) 20 7581 4646
Fax: +44 (0) 20 7584 8 481
Email: london@kazembassy.org.uk

Kazakhstan also has a consulate (which issues visas) in Aberdeen at:

10 North Silver Street
Aberdeen AB10 1RIL
Tel/Fax: +44 (0) 1224 622465
Email: kazcon@btconnect.com

The consulate is located in Aberdeen because of the close business links between Aberdeen (the centre of the UK oil industry) and Atyrau (the centre of the Kazakhstan oil industry).

In Europe, Kazakhstan also has embassies and/or consulates in Austria, Belarus, Belgium, Bulgaria, Croatia, Czech Republic, France, Germany, Greece,

Hungary, Italy, Lithuania, Netherlands, Norway, Poland, Romania, Spain, Switzerland and Ukraine (you can get full contact details of all Kazakhstan embassies at: http://www.gokazakhstan.com). Because over 200,000 German citizens still live in Kazakhstan, the Kazakhstan Embassy in Germany has seven consulates spread throughout the country.

In the United States, the Kazakhstan Embassy is located at:

1401 16th Street N.W.
Washington DC 20036
Tel: +1 202 232 5488
Fax: +1 202 232 5845
Email: kazakh.embusa@verizon.net

Its website is at: http://www.kazakhembus.com
Here again you can download a visa application. The Washington DC Embassy serves most of the southern and western United States, whilst the Kazakh Consulate in New York serves the northern and eastern ones. The Consulate is at:

305 E 47th Street (3rd floor)
New York NY10017
Tel: +1 202 888 3024
Fax: +1 202 888 3025
Email: kzconsulny@un.int
Website: http://www.kazconsulny.org

With so much information now available on the Internet it is unlikely that a visit to the Embassy itself – to chat with the Commercial Attaché (if he or she can spare the time) – would be especially productive. Reserve your energies rather for visiting the Embassy for really important matters, like getting your visa.

UK Ministries and other government agencies

However, there are of course many other sources of information and assistance in Europe and the US on Kazakhstan besides the Embassies and the Internet.

2

UKTI

Because of frequent reshuffling and changes in trade policies, the form of UK government assistance to businessfolk interested in Kazakhstan, tends to change from year to year, but, at the time of writing (2009), the place to start in the UK is with the UK Trade and Investment (UKTI) (http://www.uktradeinvest.gov.uk) whose head offices are at Kingsgate House in Victoria Street in London (switchboard +44 (0)207 2152471). UKTI helps UK businesses export and establish business abroad, but also helps foreign investors establish in the UK. UKTI has regional offices in nine English regions and offices in Scotland, Northern Ireland and Wales.

Scottish Development International

The person dealing specifically with commercial enquiries/contacts on Kazakhstan is Brian Robertson at the Kingsgate House office (tel: +44 (0)207 2144891, email: brian.robertson@uktradeinvest.co.uk) Each region of the UK has its own team of International Trade Advisers whom you can consult. In Scotland it is Scottish Development International (SDI) at SDI Headquarters, Atlantic Quay, 150 Broomielaw, Glasgow G2 8LU (tel: +44 (0) 41 2282828) that you contact.

UKTI offers the following three main services:
* Advice and Support
* Information and Opportunities
* Making it happen

They do this by providing you with the services of International Trade Advisers at your local office, by helping you to get export information and to find business opportunities (for example, tenders) in the market which interests you, and by helping with tradeshow access, joining trade missions abroad etc.

Credit guarantees

Export Credits Guarantee Department

The ECGD, the Export Credits Guarantee Department is the UK's official export credit agency which does three things. It provides insurance to UK exporters, it provides guarantees for bank loans in order to support financing of exports, and it provides political risk insurance.

ECGD's main aim is thus to help UK exporters to business overseas and to help British companies to invest overseas. New customers should contact the New

Customer Service team at help@ecgd.gsi.gov.uk or telephone +44(0)207 512 7887. ECGD's address is:

ECGD
PO Box 2200
2 Exchange Tower
Harbour Exchange Square
London E14 9GS

In 2007 ECGD guaranteed an export of Motorola telecommunication equipment to Kazakhstan for a value of GBP18 million.

Further sources of information in the UK

Other useful sources of information or contacts on Kazakhstan in the United Kingdom are at least two organisations dedicated to promoting closer links between Kazakhstan and the United Kingdom. These are the British-Kazakh Society and the Scottish Kazakh Trade Desk.

The British-Kazakh Society was founded in 2002 to promote relations between the United Kingdom and Kazakhstan. Its patrons are President Nazarbayev and the Duk of York. Its offices are at 105 Salusbury Road, London NW6 6RG

British Kazakh Society

Tel: +44 (0) 20 7596 5176
Fax   +44 (0) 20 7596 5115
Email: info@bksoc.org.uk
Website: http://www.bksoc.org.uk

The Society has more than one hundred corporate members and sponsors drawn from British business, finance and industry. Annual corporate membership costs £300. They arrange occasional meetings in London, and promote events in both Kazakhstan and the UK.

The Scottish Kazakh Trade Desk is based in Aberdeen and exists to help businesses to develop links between Aberdeen and Kazakhstan. This is because Aberdeen, as the oil capital of the United Kingdom, has already established over one hundred businesses in Kazakhstan

Scottish Kazakh Trade Desk

2

(largely in the oil and gas sector). The Trade Desk works closely with the Consulate of Kazakhstan in Aberdeen and can be contacted on telephone +44 1224 321162 or on their website: http://www.scotkaztradedesk.com

Kazakh-British Trade and Industry Council

At a more rarefied level is the Kazakh-British Trade and Industry Council (KBTIC) which is a meeting of top Kazakh and British officials who meet once a year (alternately in Astana and London) to discuss trade issues of mutual interest. This is arranged by UKTI.

The European Union (EU)

The European Union (including of course the UK) is Kazakhstan's most important trade partner accounting for almost 40% of Kazakhstan's external trade. In 2007 the value of exports to and imports from Kazakhstan was just on €20 billion and 80% of Kazakhstan's exports consisted of oil and gas to the European Union. Half the foreign investment in Kazakhstan in 2006 was made by EU companies.

The WTO

However, because Kazakhstan is not yet a member of the World Trade Organisation (WTO) most trade agreements between the member countries of the European Union and Kazakhstan are done on a bilateral basis rather than through the EU. Big countries like the UK, Germany and France probably prefer to go it alone and set up their own trading organisations, but for smaller countries, say Estonia or Slovenia, it could be tempting to go through the EU.

EBRD

Another European institution which could be of interest is the European Bank for Reconstruction and Development (EBRD) (http://www.ebrd.comn) headquartered in London. This is a major investor in Eastern Europe and Central Asia. In Kazakhstan EBRD has been heavily involved in the development of small and medium enterprises (SMEs) and in natural resources, telecoms and agribusiness. It has financed a total of 97 projects to a total value of €3.4 billion. EBRD can be contacted at its head office at 1 Exchange Square, London EC2A 2JN (telephone +44(0)20 73386000). It can also be contacted at its field offices in Almaty and Astana.

In the United States

In the United States the place to start is, of course, the US Department of Commerce (http://www.commerce.gov) and the US Export Assistance Centres within the Department of Commerce with 109 offices in the 50 states (see http://www.buyusa.gov/home/us.html). Each of these offices has from two to seven international trade officers, each allocated to a number of commercial/industrial sectors. These can:

- Get you appropriate information on the export process
- Help you identify your international markets
- Provide comprehensive and accurate market research for your targeted market
- Help you find buyers, agents, distributors, representatives, partners etc.
- Provide business background and credit checks on buyers and representatives
- Promote your products overseas
- Refer you to other qualified partners/advisers

Other services before you go

Much will depend on the size of your budget and your ambitions on how much research you want to do before you leave for Kazakhstan. However, using professional applied research is probably the next best thing to going to Kazakhstan, but it does not come out cheap.

The Economist Intelligence Unit (EIU)

The Economist Intelligence Unit (http://www.eiu.com) is a British institution which was established in 1946. It is part of the Economist Group, which publishes the highly respected *The Economist* magazine. EIU has 40 offices overseas, 130 full-time economists and analysts and about 650 correspondents providing analyses and forecasts for over 200 countries. As its name implies, it provides very high-power economic intelligence, and probably the best impartial intelligence in the world.

EIU

Its best-known and best-established product is the monthly 'Country Report' which it now produces for 120 different countries. This is usually a completely up-to-date, detailed analysis of all aspects of the economy.

2

The annual print or online subscription for the Kazakhstan report is US$610 per annum and the most recent single issue will cost you USD 285. Individual chapters of the latest report can be purchased online for about USD 21. EIU also offers the following four other services for Kazakhstan:

- The Country Forecast
- Country Risk Service
- Country ViewsWire
- Country Data

A subscription to the EIU Kazakhstan Country Forecast will cost you US$1,195 a year and will give you an annual main report and eleven monthly updates. The forecast contains a continually updated five-year economic and political forecast, reviews of business climates and a series of market opportunities. The Country Risk Service for Kazakhstan will cost you US$920 a year for four quarterly reports and eight monthly updates. It contains two-year risk forecasts, risk rating and call-up facility to country analysts. The Country ViewsWire will cost you US$855 a year and will give you a monthly political, economic and business analysis for Kazakhstan. Again, you can buy online the latest issue in single copies or single chapters of the latest issue. A subscription to the Country Data for Kazakhstan will cost you US$575 and will provide you with all relevant economic data for Kazakhstan on a monthly basis with an annual report every August.

Another interesting service that EIU offers those investigating the market in Kazakhstan is their Business Roundtables with the government of Kazakhstan. A one day Business Roundtable arranged by the Economist Intelligence Unit was held in the Radisson SAS Hotel, Astana in September 2008. It was attended by the Prime Minister, the Minister of Finance, the Minister of Energy and Minerals, the Minister of Industry and Trade, the Minister of the Economy and Budget. The fee for the one day meeting was €1,900 plus the cost of flights to, and hotels in, Astana. But, if your business is the sort that needs the ear of the Prime Minister, then it could well be cheap at the price! A new Business Roundtable with the government of Kazakhstan is planned for September 2009.

The Financial Times

This is yet another British institution (http://www.ft.com) and its Internet search engine is excellent in obtaining news (rather than opinion) on Kazakhstan. If you search for 'Kazakhstan' on the FT's Internet site you will find no less than 2,000 references to Kazakhstan with over 100 references to Kazakhstan appearing in a three month period in 2009. Most of what you find is hard fact, for example, new appointments, new investments, new loans, changes in interest rates etc. The FT also produces the occasional Special Reports (the last one on Kazakhstan was 2 July 2008) which can be read on the Internet if you register yourself (for free).

FT

The Economist

A year's subscription to the *Economist* will set you back about £120 a year and apart from 50 print editions of the magazine, you can also have access to the magazine's archives back to January 1997. This produced 369 references to Kazakhstan over a period of 12 years. Many of the articles contain interesting and informed opinion.

Dun and Bradstreet

Dun and Bradstreet Ltd (http://www.dnb.co.uk) claims to be the '. . . world's leading source of business information and insight . . .' and their global commercial database contains 146 million business records.

Royal Society for Asian Affairs

The Royal Society for Asian Affairs (http://www.rsaa.org.uk) is a learned society with its offices in London, whose membership is open to anyone with a genuine interest in Asian affairs (including of course Kazakhstan). It has about 1,500 members and has meetings twice monthly on a wide variety of topics. There you can meet kindred spirits or experts in your field of endeavour. Its library, established with the Society in 1901 is second to none on Asian matters.

Travel and weather advice

Most business travellers will be aware of the British Government's Travel Advice given by the Foreign and Commonwealth Office (FCO) at http://www.fco.gov.uk

2

and the US State Department's Travel Advisories at http://travel.state.gov The American version is more comprehensive, but both give a pretty clear picture of what to expect, and what to watch out for. It must be said that neither site would put you off visiting Kazakhstan and they make it out to be a relatively secure place to travel – which it is.

The alert business traveller is also wise to check the weather at his destination before he or she heads out. This is important in a big country like Kazakhstan where Astana can be experiencing heavy snowfalls, whilst Shymkent in the south is basking in spring sunshine. Both http://cnn.com and http://www.wunderground.com are good sites for checking local conditions in Kazakhstan.

3

getting there

getting there

The various considerations
in arranging travel to Kazakhstan

Visas and registering your stay

As far as visas and registration go, Kazakhstan has tidied up its act. Many of us who had despaired of Kazakhstan's treatment of incoming businessmen have in fact been pleasantly surprised. Compared with just a few years ago, life for the Kazakhstan-bound traveller has become a lot easier, both as far as visas and travelling are concerned.

As in most post-Soviet states, getting a visa for Kazakhstan used to be a time-consuming business. Three things have made life somewhat better on the visa front.

Firstly, there are more Kazakhstan embassies and consulates with the authority to issue visas. There are now Kazakhstan embassies and consulates issuing Kazakhstan visas in no less than the 47 countries. They are:

Afghanistan, Australia, Austria, Azerbaijan, Belarus, Belgium, Bulgaria, Canada, China, Croatia, Czech Republic, Egypt, France, Georgia, Germany, Greece, Hungary, India, Iran, Israel, Japan, Korea (South), Kyrgyzstan, Lebanon, Libya, Lithuania, Malaysia, Mongolia, Netherlands, Norway, Pakistan, Poland, Romania, Russia, Saudi Arabia, Singapore, Spain, Switzerland, Tajikistan, Thailand, Turkmenistan, Ukraine and Moldova, United Arab Emirates, United Kingdom, United States and Uzbekistan.

Countries with Kazakh embassies and consulates

Many of these now have their own website and the visa application form can be downloaded directly.

Secondly, you no longer need the official invitation; at least for a simple thirty-day tourist or business visa, which is all that most businessmen visiting the country on spec will need. In February 2008 Kazakhstan eased its visa regulations for citizens of the following 35 countries: Australia, Austria, Belgium, Canada, Croatia, Denmark, Finland, France, Germany, Greece, Hungary, Italy, Iceland, Ireland, Israel, Japan, Liechtenstein, Luxembourg, Malaysia, Monaco, Netherlands, New Zealand, Norway, Portugal, Poland, Republic of Korea, Saudi Arabia, Singapore, Slovak Republic, Spain, Sweden, Switzerland, United Arab Emirates, United

Official invitation

3

Kingdom and Uniterd States – by no longer imposing the somewhat cumbersome invitation process. For example, a two page form, a photograph, US$60 and a one week's wait will get you a thirty-day tourist visa at the Kazakhstan Consulate in Oslo, Norway. Ten years ago you had to send your passport to London, with an official invitation and wait three weeks for the same visa.

Thirdly, if you have one of these visas which do not need an invitation, you are no longer responsible for making sure you get yourself registered with the police within five days of arrival. This used to be a tedious practice, meaning you could easily fall foul of the

Police registration

immigration authorities if you did not meet the deadline. Now you are automatically registered with the authorities if you arrive at a major airport, and your immigration form is properly stamped. (Do not forget to retain the form which you will need when you leave the country again!) But if you are arriving by road or rail it is still necessary to ask your hotel to arrange for registration with the police.

If you do intend to spend more than thirty days in the country, or if you want a multi-entry visa, then you will need a letter of invitation from a sponsor in Kazakhstan

Multi-entry visa

to accompany your visa application. In fact such can easily be obtained by email from good English-speaking travel agencies (see the list of recommended ones at the end of the book) in a matter of hours. Or of course your client or employer can do it. A multi-entry visa is, in fact, often a very wise precaution. It is more or less obligatory and makes life very much simpler if you are intending to travel to China, Russia or any of the other Central Asian states during your trip to Kazakhstan.

You can in fact get a single-entry visa on arrival at the main airports, as long as you have done your homework. You have to arrange for your sponsor to issue a letter of invitation and get this registered with the Ministry of Foreign Affairs who will issue a registration number. On your arrival at the airport you go to the Visa Office with your passport, your immigration form, your photograph, the visa fee, a copy of your letter of invitation and your registration number. If the Visa Office does not have your registration number in its records, you have a problem, so

3

A round trip to the 'Stans?

A business trip taking in several of the Central Asian republics may sound exciting enough when discussed in a Notting Hill wine bar. Putting it into practice is somewhat more challenging. The problem is the visa regimes in the five republics. Each country has its own – changing – set of rules. And none seem to be geared to each other's. Getting a visa on entry still seems to be impossible, with some exceptions. This means you have to apply to each Embassy separately (and not simultaneously, as your passport must accompany each application). Say you are planning to visit Turkmenistan, Uzbekistan and Kazakhstan in one visit, this can mean needing up to four weeks in applying for visas. Of course, processes can be speeded up through express services, but at a considerable cost. And if you are flying into and out of Kazakhstan on that trip you will also need re-entry visas to Kazakhstan and Uzbekistan – in order to get you back to Kazakhstan for your flight.

Foreign businessmen do travel in and out of the Central Asian republics all the time, of course, but it does need careful planning. To avoid nasty surprises on distant frontiers, and to keep the costs down, your best bet is perhaps to find a good, reliable visa agent who specialises in tricky visa regimes. He or she can save you a great deal of hassle.

it is essential that you know you have been issued with a registration number before you head out from home. Otherwise you risk being sent straight back to where you came from.

It is not easy to standardise the prices of visas because of different country requirements and different currencies. But it seems to run out at US$60 (or its equivalent) for a single-entry business visa, US$90 for a double-entry visa and US$200 for a multi-entry one. It is frequently required that you show written proof of having paid the visa fee into the Embassy's bank, before you can actually apply for a visa.

Visa prices

3

In Kazakhstan it is very important to keep your paperwork in order. On account of its long Soviet history, Kazakhstan is, above all, a disciplined society. In other words, policemen, security guards and others in authority feel it is their right and their duty to inspect your documents. They will say so, if they think something is not in order. So whenever entering an official building or even a major private company you will be asked to produce your documents, that is your passport. In some cases your passport will be retained by 'authority' until you leave the building – perhaps as a guarantee for your good behaviour! In some cases your details will be noted punctiliously in some great register held for these purposes. In any event there is little point in protesting unless your command of Russian is good, as English-speaking security guards in Kazakhstan are unknown. In some cases if your name (in Cyrillic script) is not on the security guard's list, then you will not be permitted to enter.

Of course it is not only on entering a public building that you will need your passport. You will usually need it if you are buying an air ticket or a train ticket. In fact you will need to balance your time carefully if you are intending to buy an air ticket to Astana the same afternoon as you are visiting the Ministry of Agriculture. Both the Ministry and your travel agent will want your passport.

Residence and work visit visas

It is difficult to generalise on how to obtain working visas and residence permits in Kazakhstan as practice and regulation varies fairly regularly. Most business visitors will be able to get by on a business visa and extensions of such visas. As long as you are being paid overseas, a business visa ought to suffice. In fact many categories of foreign staff, e.g. senior management staff, seconded staff and staff working in the Regional Financial Centre of Almaty etc. are exempted. However, if it is your intention to open up a company in Kazakhstan and to employ foreign staff in it on a full-time basis, then you will need to provide your foreign staff with working visas and resident permits. If you are not used to the Soviet bureaucracy, immigration procedures in a country like Kazakhstan are pretty impenetrable, and it perhaps best to start off with the Ministry of Foreign Affairs where, at least, they are used to dealing with foreigners. You ought to contact:

The Consular Service
Ministry of Foreign Affairs
Passport – visa department, visa support sector
10 Beibitshilik St., office # 118A
Astana 473000
Tel: +7 7172 327145
Fax: +7 7172 327592
Or:
Consular Service,
Ministry of Foreign Affairs
65 Aiteke bi St., DCS reception
Almaty 480091.
Tel: +7 7272 620076
Fax: +7 7272 624045

They will be able to spell out precisely what documentation you will need and when. Apart from all personal details, you will have to provide a very detailed and convincing argument as to why a foreigner should be employed and why a Kazakh citizen cannot do the work intended. The procedure is that you have to obtain a certificate from a local department of the Ministry of Labour and Social Protection that no Kazakh expert is available for the proposed post. This involves a time-consuming practice of advertising on the local market.

However, our advice is that unless you have great patience, fluency in Russian and a lot of time to spare, it is better to turn to the expert to obtain the work visa and residence permit for you. There are numerous legal firms who can do all the paperwork and the negotiations to get the work permit you need. One company, Work Permits Kazakhstan (http://www.wpk.kz) with offices in Aktau, Almaty, Astana and Atyrau have specialised in assisting major companies like Shell, Deloitte, Maersk Oil, Baker Hughes Services and Aker Solutions in

Language difficulties

3

obtaining work permits. It will cost you money, but they will deliver the goods. There is no point in trying to learn the procedure yourself if you are not going to obtain the permit. Better pay what is required to be sure. Several other legal practices in Kazakhstan can help and a list of legal firms is set out in Appendix 2.

Driving Licences

As in most countries that the international businessperson will be familiar with, Kazakhstan allows you to drive for at least six months with your own national driving licence. In the unlikely case that you do not have a national driving licence which Kazakhstan recognises, you will have to take a test and get yourself a Kazakhstan licence. A smart move in most cases is to provide yourself with an International Driving Licence which you can obtain in your own home country, and which is valid in all countries but your own. Maybe the easiest way to get one of these is through the Internet at http://www.idlservice.com where a year's licence will set you back US$35.

Some Health Precautions

Most business travellers have the constitution of an ox. They need to in order to survive the stress, the punishing work schedules, the jet lag, the language problems, the puzzling and convoluted bureaucracy and the strange and unfamiliar food and drink. All of these are part and parcel of visiting a new business destination for the first time.

And apart from business ability, the business traveller's most important asset is his or her health. In a small town in Kazakhstan, 6,000 kilometres from home, feeling 'a bit under the weather' is really not an option. You cannot say you feel a bit strange today and that you had better have the day off to be on the safe side.

No, however bad you may feel, you have a schedule to keep to, and people to meet. You just have to get on with it. So the seasoned traveller knows that he or she has to be self-sufficient. This is particularly important in a country like Kazakhstan where few medical personnel

3

or pharmacists speak anything but Russian. Most visitors will have difficulties in explaining what is wrong, and most doctors or pharmacists may have difficulties in understanding what the problem is. Of course if you are unfortunate enough to fall and break a leg, everyone will know what is wrong and you will be hauled off without further ado for treatment. But most health problems are less serious than this and you have to be prepared to tackle them yourself. In Kazakhstan alcohol and heavy food are often difficult to avoid in a business environment. The best antidote for these is exercise and plenty of sleep. Many of the better hotels have a training centre and /or a swimming pool where you can spend a few minutes every day keeping in reasonable shape.

However, any business traveller should also take responsibility for his or her own health, by arranging regular check-ups with your doctor and dentist before travelling. In addition, carrying a blood type certificate is a wise precaution, in case of the need for a blood transfusion. Loperamed (Imodium), paraceteamol, sleeping pills, insect repellent and condoms should also be in your medical kit.

For visitors to Kazakhstan the World Health Organisation (WHO) recommends vaccinations for diphtheria, hepatitis A and B, tetanus and typhoid. Most business travellers will already have these, but, of course, it is essential to check with your doctor what the latest vaccination recommendations are for the country and which of your vaccinations need updating. Rabies can still be a problem in parts of the country although it is still a pretty rare disease, and tick-borne encephalitis is present in the mountains and forests in the spring.

Vaccinations

Otherwise it is back to self-medication. Of course if you have to take prescription drugs you will have to take a sufficient supply with you for your stay as you can be sure you will not get them in Kazakhstan. It is also important to remember a spare pair of spectacles – repairing them in Kazakhstan is not always a simple business. Perhaps the greatest threat to the daily well-being of the traveller can be the food and drink he or she consumes. Most good hotels and restaurants in Kazakhstan pose few problems, although the bacteria

3

flora in Kazakhstan can be quite different from what you are used to, and can cause stomach upsets, vomiting or diarrhoea. Diarrhoea is a common health problem caused by coli bacterium (ETEC). The infection lasts from two to four days and is usually self-limiting. Rehydration – to combat the loss of liquid – is the cure. That means drinking plain water in small amounts and often. Antibiotics are seldom needed, and, in certain cases, can prolong the problem.

But if the worst does come to the worst and you do need hospitalisation, it would be well to know that on its website, the British Embassy in Kazakhstan says:

The medical facilities in Kazakhstan are not as advanced as those in the UK. You should ensure that your medical insurance includes evacuation by air ambulance.

Medical insurance

In other words, if something really serious happens, you will need insurance which will cover immediate emergency evacuation. As far as Kazakhstan is concerned, its problem is that it inherited a rather rigid form of health care from the Soviet Union and it has not yet recovered from that. The World Health Organisation reports that the standard of care in many public hospitals is poor, because of a poor state of repair and lack of essential medical supplies and antiseptics. There are of course a great many private clinics and hospitals as well as specialists and medical practitioners. Most embassies keep a list of recommended private specialists, clinics and hospitals. Again, you have to have comprehensive insurance which you know will cover all fees and treatment.

The following private health centres are available to visitors:

Astana
The Centre of Traditional Medicine
3 Microdistrict, 1 Vavilov Street, Astana
Tel: +7 7172 351948

Tamyr Private Medical Centre,
71 Pobedy Avenue, Astana
Tel: +7 7172 394455

Astana SOS International Clinic
8 Beibitshilik Street (Grand Esil hotel building), Astana
Tel: +7 7172 580937

Meyrim
1 Syganak Street, Astana
Tel: +7 7172 794005

National Medical Research Centre
36 Abay Avenue, Astana
Tel: +7 7172 232926

Almaty
Almaty SOS International Clinic
11 Luganskogo Street, Almaty
Tel: +7 7272 581911

**Private health
centres**

Charity Clinic Grace,
159a Abay Avenue, Almaty
Tel: +7 7272 469448

Interteach Medical Assistance Centre
83 Aiteke bi Street, Almaty
Tel: +7 7272 588100

Dostar Med
28 Sechmev Street. Almaty
Tel: +7 7172 278062

UKC
Abay-Massanchi, Almaty
Tel: +7 7272 928070

Atyrau
Atyrau International SOS Clinic
River Palace Hotel,
55 Aiteke bi Street, Atyrau
Tel: +7 7122 586911

Of course, many of the bigger foreign companies in
Kazakhstan provide their own health facilities and
medical staff for their own personnel. However, if you
have to depend on private treatment, it is not cheap and
you should make sure you are very well insured for
health treatment. Signing up a year's appointments and

consultations with one of the clinics can cost you at least US$2,000. The cost for an individual appointment can range from US$10 to US$100 or more, and on top of that comes treatment.

Personal Security

Most business travellers would not be business travellers if they were unable to look after themselves. For that very reason they take the question of personal security seriously. This is especially so in 'new' or unfamiliar environments like Kazakhstan or elsewhere in Central Asia. Experience from looking after yourself in one part of the world, say Latin America, does not automatically transfer to another part.

Police

But firstly it has to be said that Kazakhstan feels 'safe'. Astana, and, to a lesser extent, Almaty, have highly visible police forces. There are traffic police everywhere and you never seem to be far from the long arm of the law. There is therefore considerable respect for the law and the police, and Kazakhstan's population as a whole seems to have inherited the Soviet penchant for a disciplined society. It is often said that the choice profession for a young Kazakh is as policeman or security officer – and there seems to be no shortage of openings.

Crime

Nonetheless, there are signs that the disciplined society is breaking down under the weight of migration from elsewhere in Central Asia. Kazakhstan is the richest of the five Central Asian states and so attracts unwelcome visitors and crime. In addition it is on one of the major transit routes for opium and heroin from Afghanistan to the West. But the business traveller is unlikely to run into trouble unless in exceptional circumstances – and the wise traveller should take care to avoid the exceptional circumstances. Get drunk in a dubious nightclub in the early hours of the morning and you are more or less asking for trouble, and that seems to be where most crime against foreigners is committed. Arriving from abroad at the airport in the middle of the night (which many intercontinental flights do) also puts you in a vulnerable position. Pirate taxis at Almaty airport have been known to extort dollars from single visitors, by

driving them far from their destination. It is therefore
very wise to arrange for your hotel or your business
partner to arrange to have you met and picked up at the
airport. Crowded railway stations or markets are not a
good idea, but most experienced travellers know to carry
nothing of value on them. If you do need to keep money
and passport on you, it should be in a pouch
under your shirt or blouse. That way your assailant
has to undress you first to get at your cash. Another
acquaintance keeps a referee's whistle round his neck,
ready to attract attention should the need arise. Making
a lot of noise is a good idea if you are attacked. Some
bloggers we have read recommend steering clear of
officious policemen on the street who may take the
opportunity of identity checks to demand a wad of *tenge*.

Getting to Kazakhstan

Before independence from the Soviet Union in 1991,
Kazakhstan was still the back of beyond for the business
traveller, being accessible to the outside world only
through Moscow. The country struggled to build up its
international air connections throughout the nineties.
Now you can fly directly to Kazakhstan, since Astana
and Almaty are connected by direct flights to, and from,
no less than 24 international destinations (see the table
overleaf). Atyrau and Aktau, the oil cities in the Caspian
can also be reached by direct flights from overseas
(Azerbaijan, Georgia, Netherlands, Russia and Turkey).
This means that you can now fly directly to Kazakhstan
from the Far East, from China, South East Asia, India,
the Middle East and Europe. The day when you can get
a direct flight from the States may still be some way off,
but by judicious planning you can leave New York late
one night and, after a trip of about thirteen hours and
an eleven-hour time difference, arrive in Almaty around
midnight the next night with a good dose of jet lag.

	To Kazakhstan	From Kazakhstan	Airline	Almaty	Astana	Atyrau	Aktau
Flights to and from Kazakhstan							
Abu Dhabi	Tu,We,Th,Sa	Tu,We,Th,Sa	Etihad	x			
Abu Dhabi	Th	Th	Etihad		x		
Amsterdam	M,Tu,Th,Sa, Su	M,T,W,F, Su	KLM/Air Astana	x			
Amsterdam	Tu,W,Th,F,Su	Tu,W,Th,F,Su	Air Astana			x	
Baku	Su	Su	Sayakhat	x			
Baku	Tu,Th,Su	Tu,Th,Su	Scat			x	
Baku	M,Tu,W,F, Sa,Su	M,Tu,W, F,Sa,Su	Scat, Azerbaijan				x
Bangkok	M,W,F,Su	M,W,F,Su	Air Astana	x			
Beijing	M,Tu,Th,F,Su	M,Tu,W,F,Sa	Air Astana	x			
Bishkek	M,W,Th,Su	M,W,Th,Su	Air Astana	x			
Delhi	M,W,Sa	M,W,Sa	Air Astana	x			
Dubai	Every day	Every day	Air Astana	x	x		
Frankfurt	Every day	Every day	Lufthansa/ Air Astana	x	x		
Istanbul	Every day	Every day	Turkish/ Air Astana	x		x	
Kaliningrad	M,Tu,Th,Sa	Tu,W,F,Su	KD Avia		x		
Kiev	W,Sa	Th,Su	Aerosvit, Donbassaero	x			
London	M,T,Th,Sa	M,T,Th,Sa	British, Air Astana	x			
Moscow	4 daily	4 daily	Air Astana, Transaero	x			
Moscow	Daily	Daily	Air Astana, Transaero		x		
Moscow	Tu,Th,F,Su	Tu,Th,F,Su	Transaero, Atyrau Air			x	
Prague	M,Th	Tu,F	Czech	x			
Riga	Th,Su	M,F	Air Baltic, Air Astana	x			
St Petersburg	W,Su	Th,M	Pultkovo	x			
St Petersburg	Sa	Su	Pultkovo		x		
Seoul	M,Th,Su	M,Th,Su	Air Astana	x			
Sharjah	M,Th	M,Th	Air Arabia	x			
Sharjah	W,Su	W,Su	Air Arabia		x		
Tblisi	W,Su	M,Th	Euroline	x			
Tblisi	W,Su	W,Su	Scat	x			
Tel Aviv	Th	F	Sayakhat	x			
Urumchi	Tu,Sa	Tu,Sa	Air Astana		x		
Vienna	Tu,F,Su	M,W,Sa,	Austrian	x			

the ground rules

the ground rules

This section takes the reader by
the hand and talks through the
nitty-gritty of everyday life, from
how to get around to how much
to tip the bell-boy. Knowledge
of these essentials provides the
confidence to go out and do
business effectively.

The currency

Kazakhstan's currency is the *tenge* (KZT). In 2009 there were 150 tenge to the US dollar and 212 tenge to the euro. In theory the *tenge* is divided into 100 *tyin*, but since 1 *tyin* would be worth US$0.00008 (or one twelve-thousandth of a dollar) the *tyin* has not been in use for several years.

In Kazakh *tenge* means a set of scales or balance. The currency was introduced in November 1993 and replaced the Russian rouble which had been inherited from Soviet times. In 2006 a complete set of new notes were introduced in denominations of 200, 500, 1,000, 2,000, 5,000 and 10,000 *tenge*. Coins of 1, 2, 5, 10, 20, 50 and 100 *tenge* are also in circulation.

There was some scepticism when the new currency was introduced, but the *tenge* has in fact turned out to be a remarkably stable and reliable currency. It is freely convertible, and there are any number of exchange bureaux in the main cities willing to give you slightly better rates than the official bank rates. They are also open all hours of the day and night. In addition, there are also many money transfer offices (Western Union, for example) where you can send or receive foreign currency, although charges vary dramatically.

Automated Teller Machines (ATMs), known as Bankomats in Kazakhstan, are available everywhere in major towns and usually take VISA, MasterCard and a series of local cards. They invariably have instructions in English. In remoter areas ATMs may not be available, so it is wise to carry enough *tenge* in cash to see you through.

It has to be borne in mind that Kazakhstan is still very much a cash society, and recent surveys show that less than 5% of Kazakhstan citizens actually use bank services like cheques and consumer credit cards. It is therefore always wise to carry a modicum of foreign currency in cash in countries like Kazakhstan where it can take some time and effort to replace stolen or lost credit cards. This is especially true outside Astana and Almaty.

Tenge

4

Stability of
the currency

ATMs

Cash society

The financial sector and the banks

Kazakhstan has been described as the financial success story of the Commonwealth of Independent States (CIS), that is 12 of the successor states to the Soviet Union. With annual growth rates exceeding 10% since 2000, Kazakhstan has been the star performer in Central Asia. This is largely attributable to its vast array of natural resources and to the high and enduring commodity prices which only began to waver in the financial crisis of October 2008.

Growth of the banking sector

The economic boom generated huge growth in the banking sector, of 40-50% per annum. The four main banks are BTA Bank, Kazkommertzbank, Halyk Bank and Alliance Bank, which control about 70% of banking assets. But, in order to relieve the pressure during the financial crisis of October 2008, the national holding company Samruk-Kazyna National Welfare Fund bought 25% of the shares of each bank. However, even so, 2009 turned out to be a year of unprecedented turmoil for the banks of Kazakhstan. Although many foreign banks, e.g. HSBC, Royal Bank of Scotland, Citibank, Raiffeisen International, Bank of Tokyo-Mitsubishi and others are present in Kazakhstan they account for less than 15% of ownership of the banks in Kazakhstan. This is in contrast to Eastern Europe where the foreign share is as high as 80%. In Kazakhstan foreign ownership has been much more closely regulated.

RFCA

Kazakhstan also has ambitious plans in the financial sector. One important element in these plans is the Regional Financial Centre for Almaty (RFCA) (see http://www.rfca.gov.kz). Its main mission is to build a financial centre for Central Asia on a par with Singapore, Hong Kong or Dubai. It aims at improving regulatory conditions in Kazakhstan and creating better conditions for attracting foreign investment. It was established in 2006 and is said to be based on an idea of President Nazarbayev. One of its main aims is to develop a securities market or a stock exchange.

Getting about

Well over eight in every ten business visitors to Kazakhstan will arrive either at Astana International Airport or Almaty

International Airport. The others are likely to arrive at Atyrau or Aktau (the oil cities on the Caspian Sea). Astana Airport is well organised, and usually well supplied with uniformed police who discourage loiterers. Almaty Airport is somewhat rougher. The American Embassy advises visitors to arrange to be met by a hotel or a travel agent or a contact, rather than trying to find a taxi. It is said that pirate taxis will extort outrageous sums, so it is well to arrange beforehand to be met either by a contact or at least by your hotel. Arriving at Almaty at 3 a.m. to be confronted by a scrum of importunate 'taxi-drivers' can be a disconcerting experience, and is one to be avoided. But the situation has improved greatly with the opening of the new airport. If and when you find an honest taxi-driver at Almaty or Astana Airports the fare to town should be about KZT 2,000 (say US$20).

4

There is no shortage of taxis in the main cities, and any hotel can rustle up a reliable one at short notice; these you can hire for a short trip, by the hour or for the day. The American Embassy also warns against using pirate taxis that you pick up in the street. The trouble is that most taxis in Almaty are pirate taxis, as many private cars are happy to pick you up and take you where you want for a prearranged sum. You stand by the roadside and simply signal at a likely looking car. You would be unlucky indeed to have a bad experience, as it is so common to hitch a ride in this way in Almaty. It is also possible to get around on the trams in Almaty, but this could hardly be described as the transport mode of choice for the businessmen. They are very cheap, very slow, very rattly but definitely a way to get to know the locals if you speak the language.

Taxis

Renting a car is also an option, but, in Kazakhstan, really only for the experienced. Driving is aggressive and minutely controlled in the city by the ubiquitous traffic police. It is difficult to say whether lack of Russian is an advantage or a disadvantage in confronting a Kazakh traffic cop. On the one hand, you can pretend (quite convincingly) that you do not understand what the commotion is about. On the other hand, you can risk misunderstanding instructions from an officer of the law and that is not wise in Kazakhstan. It is generally much wiser and just as cheap to leave such hassles to an

Renting a car

4

experienced local, and rent a car with a driver. A good driver with his own car (an ageing but trustworthy Volga) can cost you between €10 and €15 an hour – a real bargain by Kazakh standards.

If, however, you want something newer, and maybe more reliable this is what the rates are:

- Rental of Mercedes S Class (W 220) – US$30-35 per hour, airport transfer – US$40-45, trip out of Astana – US$1 per km
- Rental of Mercedes E, S Class – US$15-18 per hour, airport transfer – US$20-25, trip out of Astana – US$0,7 per km
- Rental of minivan Mercedes Sprinter, Toyota Hiace – US$30-35 per hour, airport transfer – 40-45 USD, trip out of Astana – US$0,8 per km
- Rental of bus Volvo, Ikea – US$30-37 per hour, airport transfer – US$70-80, trip out of Astana – 1 USD per km

Getting around in Kazakhstan outside the cities and between cities needs special attention. Getting around by car is not practical because of the size of the country.

Getting around inside Kazakhstan

For those visiting businessfolk who have to get around Kazakhstan, the distances can be a daunting prospect. When you drive out of Astana on your way south to Almaty and you see a road sign which says 'Almaty: 1,250 kms' you know you are in for a 15 to 20 hour drive on somewhat less than comfortable roads, and, if it is winter, a cold and stressing trip into the bargain. For shorter distances a good bet is often hiring a local car for the day with driver. This can run out to about US$100 for the day (if you are good at haggling) and can be useful for taking the day trip from Astana to Karaganda and back for example.

Trains

With such immense distances, the long-haul passenger train may then seem tempting. True, trains are relatively cheap, and they are relatively warm in winter, but they have their disadvantages too. For one thing you cannot always choose your company, which, on some Central

Asian trains, can often be quite 'colourful'. Secondly, long-distance trains are very slow. One acquaintance recently took 52 hours to get from Aktau on the Caspian to Astana, the capital, for a meeting. From Almaty to Astana the intercity express takes 27 hours. The flight takes one hour and 40 minutes. The one exception to this is the Spanish TALGO express train which was introduced between Astana and Almaty in 2006. It is known as the Ispanski (Spanish) train and travels every night between the cities in both directions, and makes the journey in 12 hours. However, it is extremely popular with civil servants in both cities and is often overbooked.

4

But, of course, there really is no getting away from air travel if you have to visit several locations in Kazakhstan – and that means Air Astana, which now dominates the national air scene. It is a joint venture between the government and BAE Systems, the British aerospace technology company. It started business in 2002 and took over as national carrier from Air Kazakhstan when that went bankrupt in 2004. Air Astana or its subsidiary airlines now offer regular flights from Almaty and Astana to Aktau, Aktobe (Aktyubinsk), Atyrau, Karaganda, Kostanay, Kyzyl-orda, Oral (Uralsk), Oskemen (Ust-Kamenogorsk), Pavlodar, Petropavlovsk, Semey (Semipalatinsk), Shymkent, Taraz and Zhezkazgan. Most of these flights can now be booked online at http://www.airastana.com

Air Astana

Flights are not cheap. The Astana-Almaty economy return fare is US$335 while business class is just over double that. The economy return from Almaty to Uralsk in the far west of the country (admittedly a non-stop three and a half-hour flight) runs out at about US$550. In fact, if your trip to Kazakhstan involves several destinations the cost can easily exceed US$1,000 or as much as it cost you to come from Europe or elsewhere. Fortunately Air Astana takes credit cards and their online booking service is fairly straightforward.

Language
There is no getting away from it. Language in Kazakhstan can be a problem. In most countries in the world a travelling businessman can get by almost anywhere with

4

either English, French or Spanish. These will get you through in Europe, Africa, the Americas, the Middle East, South East Asia and the Far East. But not in Kazakhstan.

Until only 15 years ago, the Russian ethnic group was in the majority in Kazakhstan. It is thus hardly surprising that the primary language of communication in Kazakhstan is still Russian which probably over 90% of the population can understand. Now, however, the Kazakh ethnic group has become the majority in the country (largely because Russians, and Germans and Ukrainians, have left, and gone back to their homelands).

In most countries seeking to make their way in global markets there is pressure to learn an 'international' language like English, French or Spanish. However in Kazakhstan things are not that simple. Because the Kazakhs have only now become a majority in their own country there is also great pressure on them to learn Kazakh. Kazakh has become the official language of government (along with Russian), and young people know that, without a good knowledge of Kazakh, they have no possibility of finding a job in the country's large and secure Civil Service. It is common to find young Kazakh people (often from the more Russified north of the country) who cannot speak Kazakh and speak only Russian. Probably no more than 50% of the Kazakh ethnic group speak Kazakh and those that do are mainly from the south and west of the country. So there is a lot of catching up to do.

When faced with learning both Kazakh and English, many young Kazakhs will naturally give preference to learning Kazakh which will almost guarantee them a job. This has inevitably meant that teaching of the English language has lagged behind. And it shows. All businessmen and civil servants speak Russian and can communicate with their counterparts in the former Soviet bloc, which is still an important and powerful trading network. But surprisingly few can speak English. The same is even true for hotels and restaurants, which ought to be used to handling foreigners. They are used to it, but that doesn't mean to say they know anything but Russian. A surprising number of good restaurants have menus only in Russian and you can even encounter travel agents booking international trips who have no knowledge of English. Quite how they manage that is difficult to imagine.

All this can cause practical complications for the business visitor. When Kazakhstan opened up for international business in the early 1990s it soon became clear that business could only be done in most cases through interpreters. True there was the occasional western businessman who spoke Russian and there were Kazakh counterparts who spoke English or German. However, there was always a hope that foreign companies would be able to find more Russian-speakers amongst their ranks to visit Kazakhstan. There was also a hope that most Kazakh business folk would learn to communicate in English and/or French. This does seem to be happening, but at a very slow pace. This is surprising because so many young Kazakh folk have had lengthy stays in the United States or Europe where they have been exposed to European languages – but it does not always seem to have rubbed off.

What happens in fact is that most non-Russian speakers have to engage the services of a translator/interpreter who can assist in meetings with Russian and/or Kazakh speakers and who can translate documents (not always very successfully) from English to Russian or Russian to English. More information on finding and coping with translation services can be found in chapter 5 on page 94.

Translators and interpreters

The media and communications

Business tends to be more successful in any country if you know what is going on in that country. Most visitors will try to keep up to date by browsing local newspapers and magazines. This is easy enough in most parts of the world, but in Kazakhstan, if you do not read or understand Russian (or Kazakh), it is difficult to stay informed on what is going on in the country. At the time of writing there are about four foreign-language newspapers circulating in Kazakhstan, that is the *Times of Central Asia* published in Bishkek in Kyrgyzstan, the *Kazakhstan Monitor*, the *Almaty Herald* and the *Globe*. These come weekly or twice weekly, but are often difficult to find. Some of them are handed out as

Newspapers

4

complimentary copies in the main hotels. A major drawback is the lack of good foreign-language bookshops in Kazakhstan. Your best bets are hotel bookshops – the Hyatt Regency and the Intercontinental in Almaty and the Rixos President Hotel in Astana are excellent examples of the genre. At these bookshops you can pick up the *International Herald Tribune*, *USA Today*, the *Wall Street Journal*, *The Economist*, *Time* and other US or European newspapers and magazines. Here you can also buy difficult-to-find books in English on Kazakhstan and Central Asia and city and tourist maps. RAMSTOR in Almaty also sells foreign newspapers and magazines.

But your best sources of reliable and independent political, economic and commercial information are, of course, the multiplicity of Internet sites. An essential business tool is therefore a Wireless Internet enabled laptop, as virtually all hotels you are likely to use will have Wireless Internet or at least free Internet access. The Institute for War and Peace Reporting (IWPR) trains local journalists in independent reporting in **Internet** many countries and so provides excellent unbiased **news sites** reports from Kazakhstan and Central Asia as a whole (http://www.iwpr.net). Similarly, Radio Free Europe Radio Liberty (http://www.rferl.org), despite its dauntingly cold war name, provides excellent independent information on all the post-Soviet states including Kazakhstan. EurasiaNet (http://www.eurasianet.org) is an excellent source of opinion on Central Asia and is operated by the Open Society Institute. The Silk Road Intelligencer (http://www.silkroadintelligencer.com) is very good at gathering current economic information on Kazakhstan from different sources. For more mundane factual information on Kazakhstan, like who has just agreed to build what pipeline, for example, you can use the government news agencies Kazinform (http://www.kazinform.kz) or Interfax Kazakhstan (http://www.interfax.kz). Other Kazakhstan sources in English are Kazakhstan Live (http://www.kazakhstan.live.com), Kazakhstan Newsline (http://www.newsline.kz), Kazakhstan Today (http://www.kt.kz) and Kazakhstanskaya Pravda (the national daily newspaper) (http://www.kazpravda.kz). Perhaps one of the easiest ways of keeping yourself updated on Kazakhstan in general is to subscribe to Google's Alert service which brings to you every day every mention of Kazakhstan in the world press.

There are six main Kazakh TV channels, with very little English on any of them. Otherwise any hotel worth its salt can now serve you up with BBC World, CNN, RAI Uno, TV 5 and Deutsche Welle. In fact it is not only in hotels that you can get Western channels on cable TV, but also pubs, restaurants and any flat rented by businesspeople.

TV

4

Internet

When it comes to the Internet, Kazakhstan is rapidly becoming as switched on as anywhere else. Most business travellers will have their own PC with them, with its own modem for connecting to Wireless Internet (Wi-Fi). In the smartest hotels and business centres you will be able to connect straight away and with no extra charge. Elsewhere you may have to buy time through a password system from the hotel reception so that you can get access for limited periods of time. Otherwise many hotels have what they call a 'Business Centre' but which in fact is simply a couple of PCs connected to the Internet. When these options fail then you can always fall back on Internet Cafes, which exist in great profusion in all major towns. The only drawback there is that you may not want to venture out at night away from the comfort of your own hotel.

Phones

As elsewhere in the world, in many parts of Kazakhstan, fixed telephones are becoming a thing of the past. To all intents and purposes, then, it is mobiles which count in Kazakhstan. The two main GSM companies are K'cell where you set up an account and draw on that and/or buy cards to download funds into your account, and Activ where you buy a card at any kiosk and then download the units to your account. There are, of course, numerous other companies like Kar-Tel (Beline, Kmobile), Altel (Dalacom, Pathword, Mobile-Telecom Service) and so on.

Using the roaming services of our own home phone company in countries like Kazakhstan can be an

4

expensive hobby, as anyone who has tried it will know. It is therefore smart to get yourself a local SIM card (and Kazakh mobile number) and use that on your own phone, although you will lose all the data on your own phone. A SIM card will cost you from 1,000 to 2,500 *tenge* (from US$8 to US$20). Alternatively, you can keep your own mobile operational and you can hire a local mobile with a local SIM card for about 2,500 *tenge* (say US$20) a day. Local calls from a local mobile will cost about 20 *tenge* (US$0.2) per minute and roaming calls to Europe and the US about 40 *tenge* a minute.

Courier services

All the big, internationally-reputed courier services including DHL, FedEx and TNT of course serve Kazakhstan. DHL, for example, has 23 drop-off locations throughout the country with its head office in Almaty at:

LLP DHL International Kazakhstan
1/1 Dzhandosova street
Almaty 050009
Tel: +7 3272 588588
Website: http://www.dhl.kz

FedEx is at:
EMEX LLP
38 Tulebaev Street
Almaty 050000
Tel: +7 3272 503566
Website: http://www.fedex.kz

and can also pick up and deliver throughout Kazakhstan.

Inside Kazakhstan **Kazpost** provides EMS and postal services and can be contacted at:

71 Avezov Street
Astana 010000
Tel: +7 7172 333775
Fax: +7 7172 334071
Email: alia_d@pochta.kazpost.kz

Bogenbai batyr Street, 152
Almaty 050012
Tel: +7 7272 590605
Fax: +7 7272 590659
Email: kazpost@kazpost.kz

Another good bet for courier services inside and outside
Kazakhstan is the Kazakhstan courier service Bekk
Courier Kazakhstan Ltd whom you can find at:

Office 52
Bayzakov Street 222
Almaty 050008
Tel: +7 3272 682218
Email: bckala@nursat.kz

4

A Heterogeneous People

Doing business in any overseas market means you have
to know who you are dealing with. Today, Kazakhs and
Russians make up about 85% of the national population
of 15 million (Kazakhs 8.5 million and Russians 4.25
million). Nonetheless because of its turbulent Soviet
history, Kazakhstan is still a highly heterogeneous
society, and it has always boasted dozens of different
nationalities within its borders. This may be because
successive Soviet governments (and Stalin's in particular)
tended to use the wide open spaces of Kazakhstan as a
convenient dustbin for various unwanted ethnic groups.
Thus Kazakhstan still houses a sizeable community of
Volga Germans who were shipped here at the beginning
of the Second World War when they were considered a
threat to national security. There are still about 300,000
ethnic Germans in northern and eastern Kazakhstan
today, many in prominent positions. As many as 500,000
Germans have returned to Germany since independence
in 1991. There are almost half a million Ukrainians –
you will often find your driver is a Ukrainian – who came
here due to various upheavals in the early days of the
Soviet Union. There are voluble Chechen communities,
originating from deportations in the Caucasus Region in
the 1930s, and there are almost 100,000 Koreans, most
of whom originate from the Russian Far East from
whence they were deported in the late 1930s. The
Koreans are said to be one of the best-integrated ethnic

Demographics

4

groups in today's Kazakhstan – they intermarry and rarely return to Korea. There is also a small Russian-speaking Jewish community of about 20,000 folk, centred on Almaty, but with small congregations in every major town of the country. In addition Kazakhstan houses sizeable minorities of Poles, Tartars, Uighurs, Azerbaijanis, Kurds and Greeks. And, since independence, the country has witnessed a very

The Koryo Saram – the Koreans in Kazakhstan

To the untrained eye or the first time visitor, the locals one comes across may look much of a muchness, and not all that different from the folk you would see on the street in Manchester, or Budapest or Chicago. But that is deceptive. In fact one comes upon many different nationalities with different backgrounds, even on a short visit to Kazakhstan. It is as well to be aware of this at the outset. Take the Koreans for example. To Westerners the Koreans are very similar in appearance to their Kazakh hosts, and they have assimilated remarkably well.

The Koryo Saram is the term to describe the Korean Diaspora in Central and Eastern Asia. There are about 100,000 people of Korean origin, largely in Almaty and the south of the country. They originate from Koreans deported here from the Soviet Far East in the 1930s by Stalin (who feared a Korean Fifth column in the struggle against the Japanese). The Koryo Saram of Kazakhstan has been documented by a colourful professor of Korean origins, Dr German Nikolaevich Kim, Director of the Centre for Korean studies at Al-Farabi Kazakh University in Almaty. The Koreans are now in their third generation or more in Kazakhstan and Professor Kim points out that, as a group, they have a reputation for being very hard-working, for learning both Kazakh and Russian, for intermarrying with non-Koreans and for not returning to Korea. All these traits have made it easy for the Koreans to integrate successfully into Kazakh society. One of the best-known of Kazakhstan's Koreans is Vladimir Kim, chairman of Kazakhmys, the country's major copper-mining company.

large influx of Turks. Turkey, whose language is close to Kazakh, and the two are said to be mutually intelligible, has pursued an aggressive trading policy vis-à-vis Kazakhstan. Many of the main trading houses, hotels and contractors' businesses in Kazakhstan today are owned and operated by Turkish businessmen.

4

Religion

There seems to be a widespread belief outside the country that Kazakhstan is in fact a devoutly Muslim country. Where this belief comes from is not entirely clear. Maybe it is a vague intuition that people in Central Asia are part of the Muslim world. Look at the wonderful Islamic monuments in Samarkand and Bukhara in neighbouring Uzbekistan for example. However, in reality the casual visitor will be hard put to come across many traces of organised religion at all in Kazakhstan. True, both Almaty and Astana now have spanking new mosques with no shortage of Kazakh adherents. But Kazakhstan's 1995 constitution stipulates that it is a secular state, with no special role for Islam – and, generally speaking, organized religion does not play such an important role in Kazakh society as it does in other Central Asian countries for two important reasons. Firstly, Kazakhstan is only now emerging from 70 years of subjugation under the Soviet Union, which was a determinedly atheistic state which had little time for religious practices, be they Christian, Muslim, Buddhist or whatever. Islam had a pretty thin time of it in Soviet Kazakhstan and was definitely not encouraged. In those days it was the religion (if at all) of the Kazakh ethnic minority, rather than the dominant Russians. Secondly, several scholars have argued that the Kazakhs, being a nomadic folk, never really took to any form of world religion. Being constantly on the move they never developed the religious institutions like mosques or prayer schools which are necessary to maintain organised religion. Rather they stuck to their own animistic beliefs based on the nature with which they were daily confronted in their peripatetic life on the steppe.

Nominally about 45% of the total population are Muslim (largely Sunni), 44% are Russian Orthodox and the rest are Protestants or Catholics, but religion is

4

something that is not very noticeable in Kazakhstan. Of course the large Russian minority have revived their own orthodox faith and crowds of elderly folk fill the Orthodox cathedrals of Almaty and Astana.

In 2006 the 62-metre high 'Pyramid of Peace' was inaugurated in Astana. It provides worship space for Judaism, Christianity, Islam, Buddhism, Hinduism and Taoism. It was designed by Sir Norman Foster and was intended to symbolize Kazakhstan's role as a centre for world religion.

The gender balance

In post-Soviet societies like Kazakhstan it is common to assume that the status of women is relatively high.

This is because of the Soviet tradition of educating women and because of women's active participation in the labour force. It is true that in Kazakhstan women do participate fully in society. A high proportion go out to work, although the number of nursery schools has been reduced since independence, and this tends to keep some women at home while the kids are small. Compared with Europe or America a high proportion of women seem to go in for technical or professional careers as, say, doctors, engineers and the like, and the lower echelons of the Civil Service seem to be dominated by women.

But it is also noticeable that women are not well represented at higher levels in politics or administration. In 2009 there was only one woman minister (the Minister of Justice) out of 18 Cabinet ministers and not one woman served as a regional governor (*akim*).

Life expectancy

However, one of the most striking features of Kazakhstan, which the first time visitor will not readily notice, is the big difference in the longevity of men and women. The average age for men in Kazakhstan is 61 and for women it is 72. United Nations statistics show that a boy born in Kazakhstan today has a 45% chance of reaching the age of 60, and this is one of the worst rates in the world. Even in Sudan a boy has a better chance of reaching 60. Nobody really knows why men's rates of survival in Kazakhstan are so low. It has been attributed to a poor lifestyle developed after independence caused by smoking, too much alcohol, lack of exercise, stress, divorce and lack of adequate safety measures at work. The situation is very similar in today's Russia. With working men dying relatively young (and/or being sickly) the burden for caring for any children inevitably falls on the women left behind. It is not uncommon to come across a single mother whose husband has either evaporated or become too ill to work, struggling to keep the family together.

4

Office hours

Office hours in Kazakhstan tend to be longer than those in Europe. This is perhaps more so in the Civil Service offices in Astana rather than commercial offices in Almaty. Office hours are often frighteningly long in the Civil Service. It is not unusual for higher civil servants to work from 9 a.m. to 9 p.m., often six days a week. Nor is it not uncommon for Civil Service offices to be staffed on Sundays (the official day of rest in Kazakhstan). In Astana the reason may be that many people feel they are on 'secondment' to Astana from elsewhere in the country. They often do not take their families to Astana and so live alone without much of a home life to go back to. Work therefore tends to assume greater importance. Most commercial offices work a five-day week, usually from 9 a.m. to 6 p.m. with a one-hour lunch break.

Weather

The concept of 'Kazakhstan weather' is something of a contradiction in terms. It is difficult to summarise the weather in a country the same size as Europe. Most of Kazakhstan consists of steppe and desert. Being far from any maritime influence, it is generally dry, hot in summer and cold in winter. The summer heats are tempered by low humidity, and the winter is generally dry and sunny.

Still it can be said that Kazakhstan is a country of climatic extremes. In Almaty, in the shadow of the Tian Shan Mountains, the temperature can range from -30°C in January to +35°C in June. In Kazalinsk in the west near the Aral Sea, it can range from -33°C in January to +41°C in June. In April alone the temperature in Kazalinsk can range from -12°C to +31°C showing the extreme nature of the climate. The decision to move the

4

capital from the relatively balmy Almaty to the severe Astana was not popular with the civil servants who had to up sticks and move. Astana is one of the coldest capitals in the world with temperatures of -35°C and -40°C being common. This, combined with screaming winds of up to 60 kph, makes life outdoors in midwinter a real trial to those not used to it. It is thus well to be dressed for most climates when visiting Kazakhstan. Long drawers and woolly vests are a must if you are going to be outdoors in winter.

5

getting down to business

5

getting down
to business

This chapter provides elementary
guidance on the etiquette of business,
and also contains details of useful local
organisations who can assist with the
more complicated requirements of
business transactions.

Business etiquette – the Civil service

Despite what you may see in the way of glittering shopping malls and stunning ultra-modern hotels in Astana and Almaty, capitalism is a recent and a fairly fragile blossom in Kazakhstan.

So, for this reason many of the initial contacts you will run across in Kazakhstan will come from the somewhat grey, leaden and plodding world of the post-Soviet Civil Service. Your first encounter may well be with an often unsmiling immigration officer, followed by similar encounters with Customs officials.

5

And in such a highly-regulated society as Kazakhstan it is difficult for the visiting businessman to avoid contact with government officials. Because doing business in Kazakhstan is still very much a matter for government.

Etiquette in Kazakhstan depends a lot on where you are. Kazakhstan is a big country with several different business environments. Astana is largely a city of civil servants which requires one approach, Almaty is a commercial city which requires another. In the more traditional parts of Kazakhstan, particularly in rural areas and in the south, another approach is called for.

Different approaches for different regions

Dealing with the Civil Service in Kazakhstan can be trying until you get used to it. Civil servants tend to be formal. Frequently they are recent recruits, inexperienced and often unsure of themselves. Many may never have had any dealings with a foreigner before. To get an appointment it is often not enough to phone up the individual or his or her secretary to fix a time and a date. Many civil servants will want a letter explaining what the purpose of the meeting is. Even that may not be enough. The person you are trying to get to may use the letter you sent to give you the brush-off. He or she is not the person who deals with that matter so there is no purpose in a meeting. This can be pretty frustrating as you do not get the chance to put your point to the person or to explain what it is you are after. This can also mean a great waste of time. You simply cannot put off meetings for two or three days, if you are planning a

Making an appointment

5

mere ten days in the country for the whole visit. It seems that things have changed from ten years ago, when Kazakhstan was a 'new' country and civil servants were more than happy to meet foreigners who were bringing new ideas. This may be because people have got used to foreign businessfolk, and become more confident in their own ideas.

In such cases it is best to use your local Kazakh agent or contact to try to fix the meeting in any way they can. A direct approach by a foreigner can be off-putting and is often met with refusal by a civil servant who is unsure of himself, or of his fluency in English. The prospect of meeting a foreigner can be a daunting one for civil servants who have had relatively little exposure to foreign ways and practices, and whose language skills are limited. If all else fails, it may be worth trying to get in without an appointment at all. That means convincing the security staff that you have an appointment when you do not, and, if that works, it means trying to get the person you want to see to give you five minutes of their time there and then. Practised business travellers usually know how to gatecrash as a last resort – and of course once the ice is broken things often go swimmingly.

If and when you do succeed in making the formal appointment the next problem can be the security staff at the entry to the building. Kazakhstan is very security-conscious – something it may have inherited from its Soviet past. You must carry a photo identity document, preferably your passport, which you must be prepared to leave in the possession of the security staff. No document, no entry is the rule, however important or pressing is your appointment. In some cases some Ministries seem to maintain lists of names of people who are allowed to enter the building and if your name has not been inserted on the security guard's list, Hard Luck. It is not unknown for the visitor to have to phone the person to be visited to come out of his office to fish the prospective visitor out of the clutches of Security.

Security staff

In meetings with government officials you should always direct your conversation at the main person on the government side. To ignore him/her is a cardinal sin. It frequently occurs that if you have a meeting with a high-ranking official, say a Governor of a Province, that there will be upwards of 30 people on the government side. However, no one may speak unless specifically ordered to do so by the Governor himself, so that your conversation is with the Governor himself, and anyone invited by the Governor to speak. It is unwise to address someone other than the Governor, as the person being addressed may be too embarrassed to reply. On your side too, there should be one main spokesman. Thus meetings are formal, and not chatty exchanges of ideas that you might be used to back home. It may therefore take a number of meetings to get to where you want to be.

Business etiquette – the private sector

Fixing meetings in the commercial sector is usually not so demanding – both parties usually have a mutual interest in meeting – but the formalities do have to be observed. Businesspeople in Kazakhstan tend to be more formal than Westerners – you should have a suit and tie – and things can take longer than you expect. If you do not speak Russian and you are in doubt as to whether your counterpart can get by in English, it is essential to clear this up beforehand. Either you or they have to make sure a competent interpreter will be on hand. In some cases you may be expected to pay for the services of your host's interpreter. It is always best to arrange to take your own trusted interpreter along. Almost everyone in Kazakhstan will have a business card and you will need one too, preferably in Russian and English. Otherwise business meetings in Astana and Almaty will be fairly similar to those elsewhere. Business lunches are common, and business dinners are even commoner especially in the smaller towns. These can be fairly extended affairs, and quite taxing if your hosts can take a drink. They will expect you to be able to do so too, and many businessmen in Kazakhstan, like those in Russia, expect you to be able to put away a lot of vodka. In smaller centres the choice of places for eating out is usually very limited so that you can easily find yourself eating in the only restaurant/disco/dance floor in town. Trying to converse in broken English to the amplified tones of Madonna while toasting in large tumblers of vodka needs considerable practice before getting it right.

5

5

It is therefore wise to weigh up the situation carefully beforehand before accepting invitations to business dinners. It is also wise, but not always effective, to set a time limit – you have to be in the hotel by 11 p.m. for an important international call from the boss, for example.

Traditional meals

Business meetings in rural Kazakhstan, especially in the south and west, can often end in a traditional meal of *besbarmak* (meaning five fingers) which is a vast stew of horse, mutton or lamb, onion, vegetables, broth and noodles. This is usually accompanied by a sheep's head, parts of which are regarded as great delicacies. The visiting businessman is likely to end up as guest of honour. In this position his task may be to lead the toasts and to serve up delicate pieces of the sheep's head, for example, the ears, the eyes, the cheeks to other guests. Ideally this should be accompanied by a compliment in Kazakh verse, such as '*I gift this ear to Kairat because of his ability as a good listener*'. But few foreigners seem to get that far in Kazakh. The point of traditional Kazakh dinners of *besbarmak* is the forging of business alliances

Toasts

through a succession of vodka toasts. The visitor must be prepared to toast frequently with generous compliments to his or her hosts. This can be a pretty taxing ritual. There are two rules for surviving it: drink a great deal of water to dilute the vodka, and try not to worry about your commitments the next day. It hardly needs saying that making excuses on the grounds of a tight schedule is regarded as very bad form. It is much better to relax and enjoy this magnificent form of Kazakh traditional hospitality dating back to the Middle Ages.

The business visitor's dilemma

By their very nature all business trips tend to be hectic – and trips in Kazakhstan are no exception to this. You are there to be as cost-effective as possible. To meet as many people as you can, in as short as possible a time, at the least possible cost. With hotel room rates of US$500 or more a night, the more days you spend in the country, the higher the cost. An extra week in Kazakhstan can easily mean another US$5,000 on your travel bill, plus re-scheduling your flight home, and will your visa last that long? At the same time you find that you are in a country where the civil servant or the private client is not in the same hurry as you are – in fact the business rhythms are extremely casual. '*Cannot fit you in this week I am afraid. What about after the weekend?*' And to the business visitor, public holidays and weekends are an unmitigated disaster – they produce no results, but just cost money.

So you line up an impossibly ambitious schedule of meetings, navigating through strange and unknown cities by taxi, not speaking the language, nor having a city map that you can read, in a temperature over 30°C and a humidity to match (or minus 35°C and a blinding snowstorm in wintry Astana), trying to convince the doorman that you know where you are going. And what has happened to our interpreter who was supposed to meet us here?

5

And yet you have to arrive at your next meeting, calm, cool and collected, and on time. The last impression you wish to give your host is that you are in a hurry. You must appear composed, interested and at leisure. If you give your host the impression that he or she is not important to you, or that you really have to go, in order to get on to your next meeting, forget it. Your visit has been a total waste of time. The worst thing your client knows is that sort of businessman who jets in and jets out without getting to know the country properly. And, of course, the business visitor who is in a hurry, or appears to be so, is the most vulnerable there is. If your opposite number knows that you have a plane to catch, then he also knows that you are going to have to settle on his terms.

This is the paradox and the dilemma of the businessman visiting a market like Kazakhstan. You have to give the impression to your client that you have all the time in the world and could think of nothing better than to go out for a drink afterwards, whereas the reality is that you are extremely pushed for time and are already wondering where on earth Voroshilov Street is and whether the taxi-driver will be able to able to find it and get there by 5 p.m.

But, of course, accomplished business travellers take such dilemmas in their stride. At least some of the people who read this book will already know what it is like to juggle eight different appointments in a day, having been up

5

half the night before being regaled by new business contacts with dubious vodka.

Business cards

In any country business cards are a very good idea and Kazakhstan is no exception. Since many civil servants and businessmen in Kazakhstan do not read or write English it is essential to have your cards in English on one side and Russian on the other. Such bilingual cards can be run up in couple of hours at any copy shop in Almaty or Astana and are a good investment. Everyone at a meeting will expect a copy of yours so it is smart to print off more than you think is necessary.

Finding a local partner

There are myriad reasons for searching for a local partner, an agent or a representative. You may want someone to find a market in Kazakhstan for your product that you want to export. You may be a consulting or construction firm looking for a local company with whom you can tender for an internationally-funded contract. You may be a manufacturing company wanting to find a local company who can help you set up local production of say, clothes or ceramics. We have chosen the term 'finding' rather than 'choosing' a local partner, because in many fields in Kazakhstan, the choice is not very wide so that 'finding' rather than 'choosing' an appropriate local partner is more relevant. Again, one has to bear in mind that the idea of a private firm with whom one can partner is still a relatively new idea in Kazakhstan and that many firms are still huge conglomerates, partly or wholly owned by the State.

Formal vs informal channels

In other countries – particularly in the Middle East – it is frequently possible to find partners through informal channels. You meet a chap in a bar whose best friend has just left a company which is involved in exactly what you are looking for. It does not quite work like this in Kazakhstan. Most businesses in Kazakhstan are still big, and tend to work through formal channels, and run across each other in seminars, workshops and trade missions, rather than in bars. As in most post-Soviet societies, professional workshops, trade exhibitions and seminars dealing with everything from animal husbandry to aerospace engineering have spread like wildfire in Kazakhstan (see below), and there is often no better place to strike up useful, informal acquaintances in the same field as your own. Your Embassy will have no trouble in finding you a relevant workshop, and the secretariats can usually cope with non-Russian-speaking guests.

Of course many firms visiting Kazahstan will have their own informal ways of finding suitable partners in the sectors in which they are interested. A gold-prospecting company, for example, will know better than most embassies or chambers of commerce where they would locate a suitable gold-prospecting partner in Kazakhstan, through the grapevine or through professional networks etc. But some companies do not have that luxury and have to go through formal channels to find partners. One place to start the search for a partner in Kazakhstan would be the national Chambers of Commerce which have grown up in recent years. Three of the main ones (with English language websites) are:

Almaty Chamber of Commerce
Secretary-General Nurzhan Toishy
47 Makataev Street, Almaty 050000,
Tel: +7 7272 2582099
Email: nurzhan@chambercom.kz

Their UK representative is Arthur Abdulin
Tel: +44 (0) 20 7958 31247
Email: arthur@chambercm.kz
Website: http://www.chambercom.kz

Astana Chamber of Commerce and Industry
66 Auezov Street, Post Box 1966, General Post Office,
Astana 010000
Tel: +8 3172 323833
Email: akmcci@dan.kz
Website: http://www.chamber.kz

South Kazakhstan Oblast Territorial
Chamber of Commerce and Industry, Jeltoksan Street 20 B, Shymkent
Tel: +7 7252 232477
Email: info@ukottpp.kz
Website: http://www.ukottpp.kz

5

Chambers of
Commerce

International consulting firms

5

There are also chambers of commerce and industry in Arkalyk, Atyrau, Dzhezkazgan, Kokshetau and Ust-Kamenogorsk. However, it has to be remembered that, because of the country's economic history, chambers of commerce are a relatively new phenomenon in Kazakhstan and most came into being after the appropriate legislation was passed in 2005. These probably have the advantage of being in touch with the grass roots, but in some ways they may be too near the grass roots and may be unable to identify local firms which can operate in English and within an international business environment.

To identify such firms you may have to move up a notch in standard and price to the international consulting giants like:

- Ernst & Young
- Deloitte
- KPMG
- PriceWaterhouseCooper

These all have offices in Almaty, Astana and Atyrau and Aktau. There are many new such international firms every year and all have a sizeable presence in Kazakhstan, and employ top-notch multilingual staff with an intimate knowledge of Kazakhstan's business and industry. They also have offices in your home country. They cost money but they know how to find what you are looking for.

Trade fairs and exhibitions in Kazakhstan

One of the quickest and least painful ways of orientating yourself on the business scene in a country like Kazakhstan is to sign up for a trade fair or trade exhibition. There are many advantages. Firstly, you know you are actually officially welcome and the government has to make an effort to ease your path. Secondly, you have a fair chance of meeting fellow businessmen who know something about what you are trying to sell/buy or do. You therefore have a receptive audience which it might otherwise take months to find.

5

Thirdly, as a foreign businessman in Kazakhstan you are still a fairly exotic bird, and fair organisers and secretariats will go out of their way to help. By your very presence as a foreigner you give the fair a cachet of cosmopolitanism which will go down well all round. Fourthly, fair organisers can often arrange good travel and hotel deals for foreign participants, particularly if they value a foreign presence – and who does not? It is unlikely that you will want to take a stand on your first visit, or at least without making thorough research first, but take a couple of days doing the rounds of the stands, socialising in the evenings and attending any lectures in English, and you really cannot go wrong.

And there is no shortage of opportunities now in Kazakhstan as fair and exhibition organisers have really begun to get their act together, producing attractive brochures in English, with good deals for both exhibitors and professional trade visitors alike.

The daddy of them all is KIOGE, the Kazakhstan International Oil and Gas Exhibition and Conference, (http://www.kioge.com) held every year in Almaty in early October. It gets bigger by the year and in 2008 hosted over five hundred exhibitors from about thirty-five different countries. The Conference runs over two days with about forty keynote speakers from government, industry, finance and business, and 1,000 delegates. The KITF, the Kazakhstan International Tourism and Travel Fair (http://www.kitf.kz), also held in Almaty in April each year, is increasingly becoming a focus for the travel business in Central Asia with five hundred exhibitors from thirty-four countries and over 20,000 visitors. Both fairs are held at the custom-built Atakent Exhibition Centre in central Almaty (see http://www.exhibitions.kz.showengl.html). In 2009 trade fairs for telecommunications equipment, health care, hotels, restaurants, supermarkets, windows and doors, real estate, food processing, mining equipment and technology, fashion and furs were held in both Astana and Almaty. Astana boasts the Korme Exhibition Centre, the Congress Hall and several hotels for trade fairs. International fairs are also held in Aktau, Atyrau, Shymkent and Karaganda, mainly, but not exclusively, in the mining and oil and gas sectors.

KIOGE

KITF

5

Help on the ground for businesses

Apart from the business community in Kazakhstan (chambers of commerce, trade fairs, exhibitions and high-powered corporate advisers mentioned above) there is no shortage of advice and assistance available to visitors looking to do business in Kazakhstan. In the first instance it is to your Embassy that you would go. And there can lie your first problem. Although the government of Kazakhstan decided more than ten years back that Astana is the capital of the country, not all embassies, and not all businesses, seem to agree with that interpretation. Many cling to their offices in the commercial capital, Almaty, 1,250 kms and almost two hours by air south of Astana. Some have a schizophrenic attitude and have offices in both cities.

The United Kingdom has its Embassy (and the Ambassador) located in Astana, and a British Embassy office in Almaty, which contains the visa and consular section. In fact the Embassy has three offices in Kazakhstan, since UK Trade and Investment (UKTI) has an office with two advisory staff in Atyrau, the country's oil capital on the Caspian Sea. This is not an unreasonable arrangement in such a large country. The main UKTI office is in Astana and is manned by three advisors led by the Head, Bernie Wilson. This office offers an Overseas Market Introduction Service (OMIS) which can include assistance in finding local partners. The office can be contacted at:

The British Embassy (UKTI)
Kosmonatov Street 62
RENCO Building, 6th floor
Astana 010000
Tel: +7 7172 556237
Email: bernie.wilson@fco.gov.uk

The US Embassy has a similar set-up with its official headquarters (and its Ambassador) at Ak Bulak 4, in Astana and it has a branch office in Almaty which is where many important sections of the Embassy are located, e.g. USAID, the Peace Corps, the US Consulate and the Commercial Service. The US Commercial Service is at:

Samal Towers Building, Almaty
Tel: +7 7272 504850.
Email: almaty.office.box@N0SPAM.mail.doc.gov

The person in Almaty for US businesses to contact is
Stuart Schaag, Senior Commercial Officer, and he has
a team of five specialists in his office.

Another very useful facility for US businessfolk in
Almaty is the **American Chamber of Commerce**
(**AMCHAM**) at http://www.amcham.kz. This produces
an excellent monthly '*Investor's Voice*' which is
downloadable on the Internet, and is full of valuable
information on different investment sectors. The
Chamber can be contacted at:

American Chamber of Commerce
Hyatt Hotel
Office Tower, 10th floor
Almaty 050040
Tel: +7 3272 587938

Other major European countries like France, Germany,
Italy and Spain appear to maintain a similar stance with
a presence in both Astana (where the Ambassador
usually resides) and Almaty where business is usually
more important. Another potentially useful source of
assistance for European business visitors to Kazakhstan
is the European Business Association of Kazakhstan
(EUROBAK) formed in 1999 with support from the
European Union. It has offices at 15 Republic Square,
211a, Almaty 50013. Tel: +7 7272 672 512
eurobak@nursat.kz

EUROBAK

Geographically Canada and Kazakhstan are quite
similar, having vast areas of prairie agriculture on
roughly the same latitude. Thus the two countries have
mutual commercial interests. Canada has a Canadian
Trade Commissioner's Service at the Canadian Embassy
in Almaty with a staff of three at:

The Canadian Embassy
34 Karasai Batyr Street, Almaty 050010
Tel: +7 7272 501151
Email: almat-td@international.gc.ca

5

The Kazakh side

When it comes to help from the Kazakhstan side, this can be difficult as contacts with individual Ministries like the Ministry of Industry and Trade or the Ministry of Economy and Budget Planning require fluency in Russian, and maybe even Kazakh. Here it might be better to use your local partner to gain access. He or she will find their way around a lot faster than you will. Many Ministries are not yet used to the idea that they are there to serve the interests of the public, and certainly not the foreign public.

KAZINVEST

In most cases, helping foreign businessmen wanting to do business in Kazakhstan is seen as the role of the commercial sector, of facilitators like the auditing and legal companies or of the foreign embassies – not that of a busy Ministry which may have better things to do with its time. An exception to this is the Kazakhstan Investment Promotion Centre (KAZINVEST). It was established in 1998 to promote foreign investment in Kazakhstan and to identify and present investment opportunities. At the moment is website: http://www.kazinvest.kz is only in Russian which limits its usefulness. Otherwise KAZINVEST can be contacted at:

KAZINVEST, 67 Aiteke bi Street, Almaty 050000
Tel: +7 7272 625297
Email: kazinvest@kazinvest.kz

Foreign Investors' Council

Another useful contact on the Kazakh side is the Foreign Investors' Council (FIC) (http://www.fic.kz) which is a very high-powered outfit indeed. This was established in 1998 to promote foreign investment in the country. It is chaired by the President of the Republic and members include the Prime Minister, various Ministers and top managers of the major international companies in the country in oil and gas, minerals, legal, banking and accounting businesses. As befits its nature it meets once or twice a year. However, it has five working groups on Oil and Gas, Legal, Taxation, Investment Image Enhancement and Operations, which meet regularly on matters of direct concern to foreign investors. For example the Operations Working Group has an active subgroup dealing with issues of work permits. The best

way of making contact with the Foreign Investors'
Council is through the Kazakhstan Foreign Investors'
Council Association whose director and offices are at:

Samal-2, bld.58, Block V (1st floor), Almaty
Tel: +7 7272 588066
E-mail: info@fic.kz

How to communicate

5

In the early nineties when a newly independent
Kazakhstan was opening up for international business, it
always struck visiting businessmen how cumbersome it
was having to work through interpreters and translators.
If you did not speak Russian, and few did, you needed
help from an interpreter to make appointments, and
then you needed the assistance of the interpreter at the
meeting itself, to whisper to you what your counterpart
in the meeting was saying to you, and to interpret your
reply back. You might also receive a pile of documents
at a meeting. If you were lucky they could be in Russian,
but, if not, they might be in Kazakh. In either case you
needed someone to sit down and laboriously translate
the document into English.

Those businessmen who have grown up with
international markets over the past thirty years have
witnessed the slow, but inexorable, spread of English as
a business lingua franca almost everywhere you go. If you
have to do business in Ethiopia or Malaysia or Mexico
you do not expect to have to conduct business through an
interpreter. You and your counterpart are expected to be
able to communicate in English and you get on with it.

Not so in Kazakhstan, although English is making
noticeable inroads in the oil, gas and banking sectors,
and in the business centres of Almaty. Elsewhere,
and especially in dealings with government, small
business and agriculture you will still need an interpreter
and a translator. After independence it was expected that
the business folk and civil servants would soon become
fluent in English, as had happened in the Baltics and
Eastern Europe after the Iron Curtain came down.
For some reason, it has not happened yet in Kazakhstan.
So, if you are counting on a series of meetings and

studying documents, you have to be prepared to hire an interpreter and translator. For many government meetings you are expected to bring along your own interpreter.

5

Interpreter costs

Using a consecutive interpreter (Russian/English) costs around US$200 a day, although it can be up to US$300 a day if important negotiations are involved or if there are workshops/training where long days are involved. A simultaneous interpreter, for a major seminar or workshop, will cost around US$500 per day per interpreter, and two interpreters (one for each language) are usually used. For other languages, e.g. Chinese, Japanese, Arabic etc., rates are as much as 50% higher. Written translation (from English to Russian or Russian to English) will cost about US$10 per page of 250 words, with German, French and Italian being around US$15 per page. Chinese, Arabic, Japanese is likely to be US$20 to 40 per page.

The nitty-gritty of doing business in Kazakhstan

Customs, currency regulations and taxes.

It is clearly essential for the visiting businessman to get to know the nitty-gritty of doing business in the country. Perhaps the most important elements in this respect in Kazakhstan are Customs regulations, currency regulations and taxes. Several of the Gorilla Guides in this series set out the details of these and other aspects like importing and exporting. To do business in an informed manner you have to be familiar with all of these. All these are highly relevant in Kazakhstan, but a few words of caution are needed before going into detail.

Kazakhstan is quite different from many of the countries featured in other Gorilla Guides. In these countries the business culture is so venerable, so entrenched and so well established, and your counterparts so wily and so experienced that you certainly need to keep your wits about you if you are not going to be well and truly swindled. We all know countries like that and we take the appropriate precautions, often by using agents and representatives who know the ropes and how you operate locally.

In Kazakhstan, however, things are different. Here, because of the Soviet history, the business culture is new, and certainly no more than twenty years old. Many businessmen (and women) there have not learned or adopted the finesses used by the ancient trading cultures and can be more directly brutal and unscrupulous. Like their counterparts in older business cultures they are also prepared to take you to the cleaners – but by a more direct route.

New business culture

5

Unsuccessful businessmen often find it convenient to blame 'the bureaucracy' in any country for all their ills, and their failure to make headway. But that is the easy way out. 'The bureaucracy' from Azerbaijan to Zambia is always part of the equation, and one of your givens. Kazakhstan is certainly no less bureaucratic than elsewhere. How could it be? Until twenty years ago everything, but everything – from running bus services to selling beer – was run by the government and so was part of the bureaucracy. It takes time to dismantle an ingrained Soviet system like this.

Bureaucracy

So, before embarking on understanding the nitty-gritty of doing business in Kazakhstan you should ask yourself how much time you want to waste in trying to understand the details of the rules and the regulations, which are constantly changing, and which are often subject to negotiation? And where everything is in Russian, or even Kazakh? The answer is likely to be that the broad outlines are enough. The nitty-gritty should be done by your agent, representative or legal adviser who knows the market and the language better than you will ever do.

So it is perhaps not essential for a foreign businessman to get involved in the nitty-gritty of business in Kazakhstan, unless he or she is already familiar with the way post-Soviet economies work, and also speaks fluent Russian. It is often far more cost-effective to operate through a local agent or representative. However, a passing acquaintance with the Customs and currency regulations and of how taxes work is useful.

5

Corruption or the market price for the service?

No Business Guide worth its salt can afford to ignore the issue of corruption. Corruption or bribery in business is an increasingly touchy subject for governments. With Transparency International, the Heritage Foundation, the World Bank and the World Economic Forum all probing the murky corners of international business, and regularly ranking countries on the basis of competitiveness, corruption and transparency, the issue of corruption in business is an increasingly hot potato.

Governments tend to blame the recipients of the bribes rather than the givers of bribes. If nobody took bribes, then no one would give bribes. But then the opposite could also be true. If nobody gave bribes . . . But it is not difficult to see how it all started. Here is a simple example. Back in the 1970s the overseas businessman's only immediate contact with his home office was by telex. And who had the only telex machine? Yes, it was the hotel where several of your competitors were staying – and sending telexes to their home offices too.

You had promised to inform the office in Manchester by 10 p.m. about today's dealings. So you go down to the telex operator at 9 p.m. who looks at you helplessly. 'But look how many other telexes I have to send' he says, indicating a great pile of drafts from other businessmen which have to be laboriously typed out and sent – and they were there before you. You will just have to wait your turn. No answer to that one is there? Or is there? How about if I slipped the poorly paid telex operator 10 bucks in foreign exchange to put my telex on top of the pile? No problem, sir, and have a nice evening.

Was this the price for a scarce service? Or was it a bribe? Difficult to say, and not one to question as long as you got through to the home office by 10 p.m. as you had promised, and the telex operator could put meat on the table tonight for his family. In fact, a lot of petty corruption can be put down to the vast differences in rewards between foreign businessmen and local officials. Officials have the power to impede a business transaction and the businessmen have the funds to facilitate it. Corruption is often as simple as that.

Nonetheless it is better to be forewarned. Transparency International has ranked 180 countries in their Corruption Perception Index (CPI), which is based on perceptions of corruption by businesspeople and country analysts. Kazakhstan does not come out well, with a ranking of 145th. However, there are some consolations – it is getting better, and Kazakhstan is the best (or perceived as the least corrupt) of the five Central Asian states, which may not be saying too much. A survey of businesses carried out in Kazakhstan by the US Chamber of Commerce in 2008 showed that the number one priority for business was more successful anti-corruption measures. There is no doubt that the authorities are making a serious effort to improve matters. However, any businessman who has worked abroad will know that in countries where public servants are poorly paid but also have the power to impede progress, and where foreign businessmen have the money, then corruption is almost inevitable. The best solution will always be better- paid public servants. But, as we all know, that can take time.

Still the high jinks we have all witnessed in the UK Parliament in the spring of 2009 show that corruption is very much a worldwide phenomenon, with no country having a monopoly!

CPI

5

The Customs regime
The Kazakhstan Customs Code, which was adopted in April 2003, is somewhat similar to the Russian one. In fact, Kazakhstan is attempting to draw up a common Customs Code along with Russia and Belarus by 2010, and this ought to simplify matters somewhat. A full translation into English of the current Kazakhstan Code has been made by the Asian Development Bank (see http://www.adb.org).

Kazakhstan Customs Code

Like most Customs regimes, the Kazak one is complicated and it is easy for the importer to make expensive mistakes. Your documentation has got to be just right. And it has to be in Russian. A Certificate of

Importing requirements

5

Conformity (CoC) is required to import goods, although the requirements in Kazakhstan are less stringent than in Russia. Also needed are your invoice, a packing list, an export declaration and, in some cases, a 'Technical Passport' for certain items which describes the goods in detail.

The World Bank in its 'Doing Business 2009' (referred to elsewhere) has analysed the procedures required in Kazakhstan to import a standardised cargo of goods (a standard 20-foot container) and is not impressed. It found that 76 days were required to import the goods and that the following 13 documents were required (all in perfectly filled-out order): bill of loading, cargo release order, certification of confirmation, certificate of origin, commercial invoice, customs import declaration, import transaction passport, inspection report, packing list, tax certificate, technical standard/heath certificate, terminal handling receipts and transit document. The cost was US$3,055. Only procedures in Chad and Uzbekistan were worse or more expensive.

So if this is your first time in Kazakhstan, and you want to avoid some of the above hassle, it is as well to get yourself a shipping agent of whom there are many in Astana and Almaty who are used to things and can clear your goods through Customs.

Currency regulations

The currency regulations are fairly simple and straightforward. Foreign nationals can import local currency (*tenge*) as long as it is declared on arrival, and must declare any foreign currency exceeding US$3,000. Kazakh nationals can import foreign currency up to US$10,000 as long as it is declared on arrival. They can import as much *tenge* as they wish as long as it has been declared on departure. Kazakh nationals can export as much *tenge* as they wish as long as they declare it, but any foreign currency over US$3,000 up to a maximum of US$10,000 must be declared on departure. Foreign nationals may not export more *tenge* than they declared on arrival, and have to declare all foreign currency exceeding US$3,000 on departure.

Taxes

A new tax code came into force in Kazakhstan on 1st
January 2009, replacing the former one of 12 June 2001.
There are six main taxes in Kazakhstan:

- Corporate income tax
- Withholding tax
- Value added tax (VAT)
- Income tax
- Social tax
- Customs and excise

Under the new tax code introduced in 2009, corporate
tax will be reduced from 30% in 2008 to 20% in 2009,
17.5% in 2010 and 15% in 2011. Value Added Tax
(VAT) was also reduced in 2009 from 15% to 12%. On
income tax the flat rate of 10% will remain unchanged
whilst on social taxes there will be a flat rate of 11%.
Full details of the new tax code can be obtained from
one of the many international tax advisers in the
country.

5

6

industry overviews

6

industry overviews

This is an overview of each
of the major industries of
the nation, and where they
stand today

General

It has been said that Kazakhstan possesses: '*the entire periodic table*' of mineral resources. In addition to that it has huge oil and gas reserves, enough for a further 70 years at today's rates of extraction, considerable tourism potential and enough agricultural land to feed its own population of 15 million many times over. Just under a half of the country's Gross Domestic Product (GDP) comes from oil and gas while mineral extraction accounts for about a further third of GDP.

Natural resources

6

In a world of rapidly depleting resources it is thus hardly surprising that Kazakhstan's long-term prospects look pretty good. This is especially so when you think of the country's highly strategic location between Europe, Russia, the Indian subcontinent and China. It is surrounded by resource-hungry markets, with the wherewithal to pay.

Kazakhstan's traditional economy since time immemorial had been nomadic pastoralism, that is, keeping sheep, cattle, horses and goats on the endless steppes of Central Asia. But this lifestyle has now more or less vanished. It was brutally suppressed in the 1930s and 1940s with the forced collectivisation of agriculture. In the Soviet period, industry featured lumbering, giant State-owned mining companies, many of which went into liquidation with the collapse of the Soviet Union in 1991.

One of independent Kazakhstan's greatest achievements has been to privatise its mineral industries, finding astute foreign investors, and developing its oil and gas business, which only took off at the beginning of the nineties.

Oil and Gas

Although Kazakh nomads knew of, and used, the oil which seeped to the surface in the nineteenth century, Kazakhstan's oil industry really did not begin to thrive until the 1980s. Since then three giant fields in the north-west of the country have been discovered, developed and now produce the lion's share of

6

Proven resources

Kazakhstan's annual production of 70 million tonnes (about 1.5 million barrels daily). Kazakhstan's total proven oil resources are put at 39.8 billion barrels, or 3.2% of the world's proven oil resources. At today's rates of extraction this will last Kazakhstan another 73 years.

Major oil fields

The **Tengiz** field on the eastern shore of the Caspian Sea was discovered in 1979 and has been developed by Chevron Exxon/Mobil, KazMunaiGaz and Lukoil. It has been estimated to contain between 6 and 9 billion barrels. The **Kashagan** oil field, containing between 9 and 13 billion barrels (1.25 billion to 1.77 billion tonnes), is thought to be the largest field discovered in the world in the past 30 years. It is situated offshore, in the north-east sector of the Caspian Sea, just south of Atyrau. It was discovered in 1997 and is being developed by a consortium led by the Italian ENI. It has experienced a series of technical problems and is expected to come fully on stream now in 2013. The **Karachaganak** Gas Condensate field, 150 kms east of Uralsk in north-west Kazakhstan was discovered in 1979 and is estimated to contain 1.2 billion tonnes (9 billion barrels) of oil and 1.35 trillion cubic metres of gas. It is being developed by British Gas, ENI, Chevron and Lukoil.

Of course it is not only oil and gas production which is important for Kazakhstan. Equally, or more significant, are the services provided to the oil and gas industry. These can be services directly related to production such as drilling, logging, and transport. Or they can be provision of personnel, catering and accommodation, legal and banking services.

Foreign investment

Although the main foreign interest in Kazakhstan's oil and gas business has been from the United States and Europe with Chevron, Mobil, ENI, AGIP, Shell being major players there has been a noticeable increase in interest from Russia, the Middle East and China. China, in particular, sees Kazakhstan as an important potential supplier of energy to the fast-developing regions of western China. Of course, the national oil and gas company KazMunaiGaz established in 2002 to protect the interests of Kazakhstan in the development of the oil and gas sector is a key player in all developments.

Aberdeen Oil Services in Atyrau

The Scottish city of Aberdeen has been the focal point of the UK's North Sea oil industry since this took off in the early 1970s. After over thirty years the city has built up hundreds of businesses which provide oil-related services all over the world. In that connection in October 2008 the Lord Provost of Aberdeen and the Akim of Atyrau, the Caspian oil city in western Kazakhstan signed a cooperation agreement between the two oil cities. Aberdeen already has several oil service companies based in Mangistau Oblast, and it has been claimed that there are about four hundred Scottish oil people based in Kazakhstan.

Over its thirty years in the offshore oil business Aberdeen has developed a plethora of oil-related services ranging from helicopter transport to cable manufacture and sub-sea engineering – and it is estimated there are more than one hundred Aberdeen-based companies in Kazakhstan. In a related development the Robert Gordon University and Aberdeen Business School have developed close academic links with Kazakhstan and the Kazakh-British Technical University in Almaty.

6

The oil and gas business is a highly international one with experienced expatriate personnel transferring from one country to the other at the drop of a hat, and as the need arises. However, Kazakhstan wants to ensure that its own nationals get a share of the action too. It has therefore been pushing hard for greater use of Kazakh nationals in the sector, and its work permits for foreigners have been increasingly hard to get.

Expatriate personnel

Like several other countries with large oil fortunes (Alaska and Norway, for example), Kazakhstan has started to salt away its oil revenues in a National Oil Fund. At the latest count this was worth about US$25 billion (or about US$1,600 for every inhabitant of the country).

6

Further expansion

Minerals
Uranium

Uranium was first discovered in Kazakhstan in the 1940s when Stalin saw the need to compete with America's emerging atomic weapons programme. Kazakhstan, therefore, has lengthy practical experience in the application of nuclear technology. Uranium is now mined at Chu-Sarysu between Tara and Kyzylorda in the south of the country, near Stepnogorsk in the north and near Lake Balkhash. Large-scale mining began in the 1960s and helped to build up Kazakhstan's nuclear industry. Now Kazakhstan is the world's third largest producer of uranium after Canada and Australia with an annual production of about 8,500 tonnes. In 2008 alone the increase in production was 28%. Now the country is aiming to be the number one producer in the world by 2010 with an annual production of 15,000 tonnes, and has ambitious plans for further expansion. Uranium in Kazakhstan is cheaper to mine and of higher quality than with its main competitors. The country has 17% of the world's uranium resources, second only to Australia (24%). Uranium production is the responsibility of Kazatomprom, the state-owned company with more than 25,000 employees. A clear sign of things to come was the signing in late 2008 of a strategic partnership between Kazatomprom and two Chinese nuclear power corporations. This was to assist in the development of new nuclear power stations in China and the exploitation of uranium reserves in Kazakhstan. With growing pressure to reduce polluting Chinese coal production, it is clear that cooperation between Kazakhstan and China on nuclear energy has a very promising future.

Iron and steel

ENRC

Kazakhstan produces about 20 million tonnes of iron ore a year, most of it in around Rudny in Kostanay Province in the north of the country, close to the border with Russia. This is mined by one of Kazakhstan's huge mineral companies, Eurasian Natural Resources Corporation (ENRC). Apart from being one of the world's largest iron ore producers, ENRC also produces aluminium in Pavlodar and ferro-alloys at Aktobe.

Kazakhstan's main steel production takes place at Temirtau ('Iron Mountain' in Kazakh) just north of

Karaganda at the Arcelor Mittal plant. With assistance from the European Bank for Reconstruction and Development (EBRD), the Indian steel-maker and industrialist Lakshmi Mittal bought the Ispat-Karmet integrated steel plant at Temirtau in 1995. At this time the plant, started in 1959, was one of the largest in the world with a capacity of 6 million tonnes, but in 1995 it was on its last legs, run down and dilapidated. It produced 2.5 million tonnes of steel and was making huge losses. Within ten years Mittal and a team of Indian experts had turned the loss-making plant around, and

Lakshmi Mittal

6

Lakshmi Mittal – Steelman

Lakshmi Mittal is perhaps now best known in Europe for being one of the world's richest men, worth upwards of US$50 billion. His fortune is built on hardnosed business acumen. *Time* magazine has compared him with Andrew Carnegie, the legendary Scottish-American steel magnate. Mittal, who is still not yet 60, has built up the world's largest steel conglomerate, Arcelor Mittal which employs 320,000 people in 60 countries. He now lives in London but was born in India, and was an early starter having founded the Mittal Steel Company at the age of 26. His speciality, and the basis for his phenomenal success, has been to turn around state-owned loss-making steel companies. He had already had triumphs in Indonesia, Trinidad and Tobago, Mexico, Canada and Germany before he found the ailing Ispat-Karmet plant in Kazakhstan.

The Ispat-Karmet complex in Kazakhstan must have been a daunting prospect even for Lakshmi Mittal as it was a State-owned behemoth which had been losing money for years. The safety and environmental records were appalling. At the same time the company provided all sorts of uneconomic services to its huge labour force, making it one of the least efficient workforces in the country. It is true to say that Mittal has transformed the economic fortunes of one of Kazakhstan's most important regions, Karaganda Province, in the course of a single decade.

plans are now to double today's production of 5 million tonnes. If you visit Temirtau today you will be taken aback to see the great ranks of chimney stacks belching out fumes into the still steppe air, but in fact the company has greatly reduced pollution and improved worker safety – and made good money. The plant and its associated coal mines in Karaganda Province now employ over 45,000 people.

Coal mining

Manufacturing of steel without easily available resources of coal is unthinkable and the co-occurrence of coal and iron around Karaganda City was the basis for the huge industrial complexes in that Province. Ispat-Karmet, the steel-maker, produces 7 million tonnes of coal a year from mines in the Karaganda Basin to serve the Temirtau Steelworks. The coal-mining industry in Karaganda has unhappy resonances as it was built up through the use of forced labour from the eleven great penal settlements or 'gulags' located around Karaganda City by Stalin between 1930 and 1950. Many of the deportees' descendants, Poles, Russians, Latvians and Ukrainians, still live in Karaganda. However, Karaganda Province has been outstripped by the huge open-cast Bogatyr Mine in the Ekibastuz coal basin in Pavlodar Province. This is actually the world's largest coalmine with an annual production of 42 million tonnes a year. Most of this is used for coal-fired power stations in the region, but a sizeable portion is exported by rail to Russia and Ukraine. Kazakhstan as a whole has coal reserves of 30 billion tonnes – enough to last it for 300 years at today's rates of extraction – and produces about 90 million tonnes a year.

Chromite

This is a mineral derived from chromium ore, and is used in the manufacture of stainless steel where resistance to oxidation and corrosion is important. In 2006 Kazakhstan was the second largest chromite producer (together with India) in the world after South Africa. Kazakhstan produces 3.6 million tonnes, largely in the major mines round Aktobe in the north of the country. The major producer is Kazkhrom. It has huge untapped reserves of chrome ore (enough for over one hundred years at today's rates of extraction) and Kazakhstan is certain to retain its position as one of the top producers in the world since over one third of the world's known reserves of chromium are to be found in Kazakhstan.

Copper

The first copper production in Kazakhstan started in 1930 at Balkhash. With an annual production of 400,000 tonnes of copper, Kazakhstan is now one of the world's major copper producers. Kazakhmys, a private company, now listed on the UK Stock Exchange, is the largest producer in Kazakhstan, and is one of the top ten copper companies in the world. It has 20 major copper mines in Balkhash, Zhezkazgan and Karaganda, as well as two smelters and ten concentrators. As by-products Kazakhmys also produces zinc, silver and gold which account for 25% of its revenue.

Kazakhmys

6

An English miner in the Alti Mountains – Philip Ridder

Not a lot seems to be known about Philip Ridder except that he was an English mining overseer employed by a Russian family in the late eighteenth century to prospect for minerals in the remote Altai Mountains, in eastern Kazakhstan close to today's border with China. In 1784 Ridder seems to have struck it rich. He discovered extensive gold, lead, copper and silver deposits in the northern Altai Mountains. Lead and zinc are still processed there to this day – more than two hundred years after he first visited the area. The mines became known as the Ridder mines, as did the local town which kept the name until 1941 when it was renamed Leninogorsk. However, in 2002 the municipal council of the town, which has about 70,000 inhabitants, changed the name back to the original name of Ridder. Whether this was because the city fathers were proud of Ridder, or just fed up with Lenin, is not known. Ridder is still an important mining centre, and has a railway connection to the Turk-Sib Railway. Thus an eighteenth century Englishman is still commemorated in the name of a town in eastern Kazakhstan.

6

Lead and zinc

Only Australia, the USA and Russia have greater reserves of lead and zinc than Kazakhstan. It is therefore a leading lead and zinc exporter from its mines in East Kazakhstan at Ridder, Ust-Kamenogorsk and Zyrianovsk. The main producer is Kazzinc the majority of whose shares have been bought by the Swiss mining company Glencore International. Lead production is about 90,000 tonnes a year and zinc production 300,000 tonnes. Over 50% of Kazzinc revenue comes from zinc and only 14% from lead. Kazakhmys is also an important player in the production of lead and zinc.

Titanium

Titanium is a very light and very strong metal whose properties make it sought after in the aerospace industry. It makes up a sizeable part of the weight of the new Boeing 787 and the F-35 Joint Strike Fighter. In 2008 the European Aeronautic Defence and Space Company (EADS), which manufactures the Airbus, signed a billion dollar deal with Kazakhstan for the supply of titanium sponge from the Ust-Kamenogorsk Titanium and Magnesium Plant (UKTMP). This is said to be the only fully-integrated titanium producer in the world from mining through titanium sponge to semi-finished titanium products. In 2007 Kazakhstan produced 25,000 tonnes of titanium sponge or about 18% of world production. As 80% of the market for titanium products is in the aerospace business the prospects are fairly bright, as the market for aerospace is likely to increase, as is the proportion of titanium used in new aircraft.

Bauxite and aluminium

In terms of reserves, Kazakhstan has the world's tenth greatest reserves of bauxite, which is used in aluminium production. The country produces 4.5 million tonnes of bauxite in Pavlodar Province close to the main aluminium smelter in the country operated by Aluminium Kazakhstan. This company, a private one, is one of the top ten alumina producers in the world, delivering about 1.8 million tonnes of alumina per annum. At the end of 2007 the Eurasian Natural Resources Corporation (ENRC) opened the first state-of-the-art aluminium smelter in Pavlodar with a capacity of 250,000 tonnes for the year 2011.

Nickel and cobalt

Kazakhstan has substantial nickel and cobalt resources in Aktobe and Kostanay Provinces. There have been recent reports of a major South African investment in nickel mining and processing at Shevchenko in Kostanay Province. A major new cobalt mining project is scheduled to start up at Kempirsai in Aktobe Province.

Gold and silver

Gold is known to have been in use in Kazakhstan for at least three thousand years, from the magnificent golden Scythian jewellery from the Altai Mountains in the east

6

Mineral	Kazakhstan Production	World's Leading Producer
Bauxite	4.7 m. tonnes	Australia: 61.8 m. tonnes
Aluminium	1.5 m. tonnes	Australia: 18.3 m. tonnes
Arsenic	1,500 tonnes	China: 30,000 tonnes
Asbestos	300,000 m. tonnes	Russia: 925,000 tonnes
Barytes	270,000 m. tonnes	China: 4.6 m. tonnes
Cadmium	2,000 tonnes	China: 4,600 tonnes
Chromium	3.4 m. tonnes	South Africa: 7.4 m. tonnes
Coal	96 m. tonnes	China: 2,062 m. tonnes
Copper	459,000 tonnes	Chile: 5,360,000 m. tonnes
Gold	10,000 kg.	South Africa: 272,000 kg.
Iron Ore	20 m. tonnes	China: 588 m. tonnes
Crude Steel	4.2 m. tonnes	China: 422 m. tonnes
Lead	62,000 tonnes	China: 1,251,000 tonnes
Magnesium	21,000 tonnes	China: 525,000 tonnes
Manganese	2.2 m. tonnes	China: 6.0 m. tonnes
Crude Petroleum	65 m. tonnes	Saudi Arabia 514 m. tonnes
Silver	810,000 kg.	Peru 3,470,000 tonnes
Uranium	5,279 tonnes	Canada: 9,862 tonnes
Zinc	366,000 tonnes	China: 2,996,000 tonnes

Kazakhstan's Main Minerals and the World's Leading Producers

Source: 'World Mineral Production 2002-2006', British Geological Survey, 2008

of the country. Gold deposits are known to be around 1,500 tonnes, mainly near Astana and Karaganda. Current gold production is about ten tonnes a year, but could be increased to 50 tonnes a year. Kazakh silver jewellery is also world renowned and comes from the country's own production. Kazakhstan is the tenth largest silver producer in the world with 22.7 million ounces. New mines are being opened around Ust-Kamenogorsk in East Kazakhstan Province.

Two important institutions

Samruk-kazyna

Samruk-Kazyna is a state holding company formed to manage strategic state assets. It is said to have been inspired by the Singaporean state holding company Temasek. It participates in state-owned companies in order to bring added value. It concentrates on the oil, energy, transport and telecommunications sectors. As such it now has interests in KazMunaiGaz, Kazakh Telecom, Kazakhstan Temir Joly (the Kazakhstan Railways Corporation) and KEGOC, the Kazakhstan electrical grid company. Recently Samruk-Kazyna has become involved in new investment projects, notably the Balkhash thermal-power station and a locomotive assembly plant in Astana.

FIC

Foreign Direct Investment (FDI) is of great significance for an emerging open economy like Kazakhstan. Kazakhstan witnessed a phenomenal growth in FDI between 2000 and 2007 when it grew from US$1,283 million to US$10,259 million. This was largely due to investments in minerals and the oil sector. It also put Kazakhstan ahead of developed economies like the Czech Republic, Slovakia, Croatia and Morocco in terms of the amount invested, and on the same level as Egypt (which has a population five times the size of Kazakhstan). The Foreign Investors' Council (FIC): http://www.fic.kz, is one of the most important official bodies in Kazakhstan. It is chaired by President Nazarbayev and has nine members from Kazakhstan including the Prime Minister and the Foreign Minister. It has 24 foreign members.

Agriculture

Take a window seat on the late afternoon flight out of
Astana to Frankfurt and you will soon see just how
much agricultural land Kazakhstan possesses. Almost
immediately you are flying over seemingly endless
swathes of wheat and cereal fields as far as the eye can
see. At the other end of the country drive westwards
from Uralsk the 150 kilometres to the Karachaganak
oil and gasfields and you will have the same experience.
Great empty fields with not a lot going on, stretching
in all directions to the horizon. In fact, Kazakhstan has
more arable land per person (1.47 hectares) than
anywhere else in the world except Australia. And it
certainly has more empty arable land than anywhere else
in the world.

About one tenth of the country (250,000 km^2), most
of it in the north along the border with Russia, is well
suited to growing wheat and other cereal crops like rye,
oats and barley. Much of the rest is dry pastureland,
ideal for the low-density nomadic, herding economy on
which the traditional Kazakh culture was based. This is
said to be ideal sheep-rearing country and very similar to
the great expanses of the Australian Outback.

It was in the early 1950s that the irascible, but visionary,
Soviet leader Nikita Khrushchev saw the potential of the
north Kazakh steppe for producing wheat. He therefore
called on the Soviet leadership to develop what he called
'the Virgin Lands' (this is 'Tselina' in Russian from
which Astana got its former name of Tselinograd),
and 'virgin' indeed they were, being largely unoccupied
steppe land in northern Kazakhstan and southern
Siberia. By 1955 as much as 350,000 km^2 (an area
40% greater than the whole United Kingdom) had
been ploughed up to produce wheat. As many as half
a million eager young pioneers, mainly Russians and
Ukrainians flocked to northern Kazakhstan to lend a
hand. Millions of their descendants remain in northern
Kazakhstan to this day and still make up the majority of
the local population. One interesting relic of the Virgin
Lands campaign is the luggage tag on your bags when
you fly to Astana. The tag is TSE for 'Tselinograd' which
is the former name of Astana, and still the airport code
for Kazakhstan's new capital. Tselinograd means 'Virgin

"Virgin Lands"

6

Lands City' because Astana was the capital of the Virgin Lands.

The black chernozem soils (similar to those in Ukraine) of northern Kazakhstan are very fertile, and the dry climate encourages production of a special durum wheat, well suited to pasta manufacture. However, the whole of northern Kazakhstan has a low rainfall (about 500 mm a year) and is subject to periodic drought, so that production can vary greatly from year to year.

At first the Virgin Lands campaign was a great success, yielding over 40 million tonnes of wheat a year, and out-producing the West, as had been Khrushchev's primary goal. However, poor planning and uncertain weather saw a fall in production in the 1970s and the 1980s and when Kazakhstan became independent in 1991 many ageing 'Young Pioneers' went back to Russia. Things were not improved after independence with the collapse of the Soviet collective farming system. This explains the great empty fields you still see today. Farming in this sort of prairie landscape has to be on a grand scale. The great distances and vast areas involved call for a highly mechanised and highly-capital intensive system. There is no place here for the small-time farmer with his horse and cart. When the collective farms went to the wall, nobody was left to maintain the tractors or the combine harvesters, and the countryside is still littered with the dilapidated remains of hundreds of kolkhoz. In many ways Kazakhstan has had to start again from square one in the Virgin Lands.

Wheat production

However, since the start of the new millennium, wheat production has been making a comeback, with a lot of support from the US and Canadian wheat business. Annual production of wheat and barley has now reached 20 million tonnes of which about 6 million tonnes is exported. Kazakhstan is one of the four top wheat-flour exporters in the world. Farms are owned and run by a few large Kazakh companies which farm, process, distribute and export grain. Farms are huge and can run up to 100,000 hectares (that is 1,000 square kilometres) or even more. Yields are around 1 tonne per hectare and with a world wheat price ranging between US$200 and US$400 a tonne it is clear that the big farms of northern

Kazakhstan (with low unit operating costs) have the potential for being money-spinners. There seems to have been considerable foreign interest in Kazakhstan's agricultural potential, and the United Arab Emirates, which imports 85% of its food, has been negotiating with Kazakhstan to invest in agricultural production. This is part of the Emirates' strategy to diversify its food sources in the face of rising world food prices. Once word gets around about Kazakhstan's wide open (and empty) spaces, it is likely that foreign interest in investing in food production will intensify greatly.

Manufacturing

In addition to the wealth of minerals which made Kazakhstan convenient as a manufacturing base, the Soviet state also saw benefits to relocating industry away from the threat of military attack in western Europe. In Soviet times Kazakhstan specialised in metal and metallurgical industries like iron and steel manufacture. Ispat-Karmet (see above) iron and steel complex served as a base for dozens of metal industries around Karaganda. Under Soviet rule, Kazakhstan produced heavy equipment like cables, rolled steel, railway wagons and locomotives, heavy agricultural equipment, tractors and excavators. Many industries had great problems with the transition from a Soviet command economy (where raw materials and markets were guaranteed) to a cut-throat capitalist one. When the Soviet Union fell apart producers suddenly found their sources of raw materials and their markets originally in another Soviet republic, now behind a wall of tariffs and Customs boundaries in a new sovereign state. For example, tractor manufacturers suddenly found it very difficult to source tractor parts from their usual suppliers in Belarus. Similarly, they found it very much more difficult to export the tractors to traditional markets in, say, neighbouring Uzbekistan who had set up tariff barriers. This tendency resulted in the loss of thousands of jobs in the manufacturing sector, and of the emigration of thousands of Russian and German technical personnel from Kazakhstan.

It is only now after 18 years of independence that Kazakhstan's manufacturing sector is getting on its feet

Transition from Soviet Command Economy to Capitalisation

6

again. One promising sign is the emergence of small businesses aiming at the local market, e.g. clothes manufacture, food processing and many other service industries. This has been greatly aided by the fostering of local banks and the development of financial facilities for small and medium-scale enterprises (SMEs) through small loans. Despite having been submerged for more than seventy years in a Soviet-style economy, Kazakhstan's citizens have proved themselves adept at taking to the theory and practice of small business.

Emergence of small businesses

Tourism

In Soviet times very little was known of Kazakhstan as a tourist destination and the only access to the country for foreign tourists was through a long domestic flight from Moscow (and you needed both a visa and specific permission to visit Kazakhstan, not least because of its many 'strategic' sites). In 1989 just before independence there was probably only one hotel of roughly international standard in the country: the 26-storey Intourist 'Kazakhstan Hotel' which, greatly transmogrified, still proudly dominates the downtown skyline of Almaty. Then tourists were not particularly welcome. It has therefore been a long haul since 1991 to build up the country's tourism infrastructure.

But what has Kazakhstan to offer the international tourist? It has the cachet of being a 'new', exotic Central Asian destination like Kyrgyzstan and Uzbekistan – but because Kazakhstan has such a huge land area, tourist attractions tend to be few and far between. There is no getting away from the fact that a very large chunk of Kazakhstan consists of flat, featureless steppe or semi-desert. Right in the middle of the barren landscape of the steppe is the Baikonour Cosmodrome (this barren landscape is good for retrieving spacecraft, but not for much else). The twelfth-century Khoja Ahmed Yasawi Mausoleum in southern Kazakhstan with its ribbed turquoise tiled dome is one of the finest Islamic buildings anywhere in the world. It rivals anything in the better-known Samarkand and Bukhara in neighbouring Uzbekistan – but in Kazakhstan it is the only one of its kind, and not easy for the casual tourist to get to. It is 18 hours by train from Almaty and 4 hours from Shymkent.

Khodja Ahmed Yassaui Mausoleum

Almaty, the former capital, and still the commercial hub of the country is, of course, well worth a visit with its dramatic site in the shadow of the Tian Shan Mountains, but few other Kazakh cities merit travelling halfway round the world to see.

Tian Shan Mountains

What Kazakhstan has to offer is its magnificent and unspoilt Altai and Tian Shan Mountains ranging from 5,000 metres to 7,000 metres on the eastern and southern borders of the country, the largely unknown glories of the Kazakh steppe, and a fascinating plant and bird life. It also has the music, the poetry, the literature, the dance and the material culture of the Kazakh nation.

6

Neither the steppe nor the mountains are especially accessible from the main centres of population, although it is not difficult to get into some magnificent Central Asian mountain environments within a couple of hours of Almaty. To experience the pristine steppe needs a fair bit of driving from Astana, the capital, and good accommodation is very hard to come by. Thus tourism in Kazakhstan is still for the enthusiast. For those who want to find the critically endangered bird species, the sociable lapwing, thought to be almost extinct before being found recently in eastern Kazakhstan, or folk who want to experience the rare Grieg and Kaufman tulips which still grow in small communities near Zhambyl in southern Kazakhstan. Such tourists are prepared to spend long hours in the field and to put up with mediocre accommodation or worse, and to pay for it as well.

Specialist tours from all over the world cater for such travellers who are usually willing to put up with a lot, and to pay well for their enthusiasms. It is therefore difficult at this stage to judge what sort of future the tourism business in Kazakhstan is going to have. What does seem to be certain is that the business-travel trade in the form of good hotels, restaurants and transport (air travel and car hire) has a sound future as business folk from all around the world hasten to Kazakhstan to participate in the development of its oil, gas, minerals and agriculture.

7

how to set up a permanent operation

7

how to set up a permanent operation

The aim of this section is to provide a sweeping overview for the visitor who is considering the possibility of a local office. Here are some of the pitfalls and benefits, an insight into the legal situation, and some of the major issues to be considered, such as recruiting, finding premises, etc.

In the beginning

In doing business overseas you need to know how to get started, what sort of company you need to set up, how to establish it, what concessions you can get, what sort of taxes you can expect and how to employ staff. This chapter will address these matters.

Many companies get their first start in a country like Kazakhstan through an export order, or through a consulting contract. In cases like these there is rarely any need to set up a permanent operation. An exporter can always export his goods through a local agent or importer whom he can often find through his Embassy or Trade Council. Through his own network of contacts, a consultant, designing, say, a road, can usually find a local joint-venture partner (he is often obliged to do so through the terms of his contract) who can help him carry out the work, organise visas and work permits for expatriate staff, find offices, buy equipment, employ local staff and pay taxes. Most companies with any experience of international business know how to find local partners in their particular sector who will help to make life easier for themselves.

But hopefully, as things get bigger, you will need to establish a more permanent local presence in the country. This is where you need to begin to understand the system yourself, and to engage the services of experts.

Choosing your form of business

Depending on your requirements, and what you want to do in Kazakhstan, there are several options open to you in the form of the business you want to establish. These are:

- A representative office
- A general partnership
- A limited partnership
- A limited liability partnership
- An additional liability partnership
- A joint-stock company

The representative office is not a Kazakh legal entity but it represents a foreign company in Kazakhstan. It cannot generate income in Kazakhstan, unlike a branch office which can do so. The other forms of business listed

7

above are Kazakh legal entities, and it is clearly best if you seek legal advice to find out which form suits your needs best.

How to start a permanent operation

Doing business overseas is never straightforward – that is why books like this one exist – and Kazakhstan is no exception to this rule. As the previous chapter on Industry Overviews shows, Kazakhstan has enormous potential and, because of this, will always be very promising indeed as a place to set up a business, to sell things to and to export things from. But . . . straightforward it is not.

Of course much of the lore on how to do business in a country comes from the 'Old Hands' – those expatriates who have been in a country for a generation or more, and have seen and experienced everything, and more, that could befall any newly-arrived businessman. They are full of endless anecdotes to illustrate how to handle the locals, how to negotiate a deal, how to make a quick buck – in a word – how to do business.

The only trouble in Kazakhstan is that there really are no Old Hands to fall back on. Before 1991 business in Kazakhstan was usually done with some anonymous state trading house in Moscow. Even after independence it took many years for private business to get on to its feet.

Most of the Old Hands in Kazakhstan are therefore relatively New Hands – few have been in the country for more than ten years, and none more than twenty years. Kazakhstan has tended to be a place where foreigners stayed a few years and then moved on. In a country like Kazakhstan which focuses on extractive industries like the oil or mineral businesses, foreigners often help to set up operations, get them going and then move to a new theatre of action.

Of course a body of knowledge has grown up, but most of the expatriates in Kazakhstan you meet are on relatively limited contracts and only the really big boys

7

like the oil companies or the mining firms tend to set up their own operations in Kazakhstan, and appear to be planning to stay in the country for the duration. Most others are like consulting companies who come in for the one contract and then decamp. The short-stayers have to do it the hard way, to start from scratch, find out how to set up an office, how to obey the labour laws, how to handle taxes and how to repatriate funds.

Using local help

As in most countries it is wise to set up a local company in Kazakhstan if you can. This usually makes life a lot simpler if you are intending to hire labour, buy property, tender for contracts, pay taxes, import or export goods and so on. However, if you are coming to Kazakhstan to set up an operation and start your own local company you are very well advised to find yourself an agent, a representative, or a good old-fashioned 'fixer'. Not to 'grease palms' or make officials more compliant, but to weave one's way around the truly complex regulations, usually only available in Kazakh or Russian, but sometimes in awfully translated English. Indeed the fact that all documentation is in Kazakh and/or Russian makes it almost essential that you go through a local on setting up a presence in Kazakhstan. Of course, things are not that simple in Kazakhstan. As anyone who has ever tried to transact business abroad, or even tried to buy a house there, will know, there are 'fixers' and there are 'fixers'. In the long run what you really need is a notary or a good lawyer. Someone who can guarantee that what you are doing is legal. It may cost a lot, but that is the price of doing business in a country with a post-Soviet legacy, and where English is the third language. In Kazakhstan, unless you are fluent in Russian, you will have to find an international legal firm which works in Russian, Kazakh and English. That ought not to be difficult. There are at least twenty international legal firms practising in Kazakhstan in Aktau, Aktobe, Almaty, Astana and Atyrau. These are listed in Appendix 2. Almost 90% operate out of Almaty and there are only three major legal firms in Astana. Several of them are associated with parent companies in the US or Europe. Most legal firms will have their own authorised translators on board. Alternatively

7

Agents,
representatives
and fixers

one could use the services of any of the main auditing/tax/investment advisors in Kazakhstan such as Deloitte, Ernst & Young, Intercomp Kazakhstan, Kazakhstan Facilitators, KPMG, PriceWaterhouseCooper etc.

Doing business in Kazakhstan 2009

World Bank – ease of doing business

7

For the past six years the World Bank has published annual reports on how easy, or how difficult it is to do business in 181 different countries (including Kazakhstan). See http://www.doingbusiness.org The Bank investigates which regulations enhance doing business and which ones constrain doing business. A set of indicators is then drawn up allowing us to compare the ease or difficulty of doing business in different countries. Countries are then ranked and the variations between countries are enormous. In each country the World Bank employs a great array of local talent to compile the indicators, and in Kazakhstan no less than 42 different individuals/companies assisted in compiling the Country Report on Doing Business in Kazakhstan.

In the Democratic Republic of Congo it takes 155 days and 13 different procedures to start a business. In Singapore it takes four days and four procedures to do the same thing. In Guinea-Bissau it takes 211 days and nine different procedures to register a property. In Saudi Arabia it takes two days and two procedures to do the same thing. In Russia it takes 704 days and 54 different procedures to deal with a building permit. In New Zealand it takes 65 days and seven procedures to do the same thing. Nobody seems to know just why these differences occur, but part of the idea is to shame the poor performers into improvement, and this certainly seems to work.

How does Kazakhstan fare in comparison? Well, not too badly actually, and things are getting better! In 2008 it was 80th out of 181 countries in the ease of doing business. In 2009 it had moved up ten places to 70th. According to the World Bank, Kazakhstan is not too bad on starting businesses, good on employing workers, not at all bad on registering property, not too bad on getting credit, not bad on protecting investors, paying taxes and enforcing contracts. However, it ranks very close to the bottom on dealing with construction permits and on trading across borders. It needs 231 days and 38 different procedures to deal with a building permit, and it needs eleven documents to export goods and 89 days to export them. To import them is almost as bad. It needs 13 different documents and 76 days to import goods. In Singapore it takes four documents to export goods and five days to export them. Of course many and complex procedures are what create corruption. Reducing and simplifying procedures reduces corruption which is a major aim of the World Bank

So businessmen visiting Kazakhstan have been warned! If the World Bank figures are to be believed (and why not?), most procedures are OK and as good as, if not better than, elsewhere, but, if you are planning on getting a building permit or importing or exporting, get yourself a good agent. It looks as if you are going to need one. One thing is certain, however, and that is that once the authorities in Kazakhstan learn how poorly they perform on construction permits and trading across borders, there will be tremendous pressure on them to get their act together and improve things. You can almost guarantee that by next year, things will have got better!

The World Bank has studied in very great detail what it means to do business in Kazakhstan, and has charted every single step necessary (and what it costs) to start a business, to employ workers, to register property, to get credit, to seek protection, to get a construction permit, to pay taxes, to enforce a contract and to trade across borders. This is invaluable to the intending investor in Kazakhstan. Needless to say, there is also a plethora of detailed and practical advice for potential investors on the Internet, and tax and investment advisers like Ernst & Young and legal advisers like Baker and McKenzie provide very useful – and downloadable – free advice. The main legal advisers are:

Other sources of advice

- Denton Wilde Sapte
- Chadbourne & Parke LLP
- Dewey and Leboeuf
- GRATA Law Firm
- Salans,
- White and Case

- Michael Wilson & Partners
- Lebouef, Lamb, Greene & MacRae
- Bracewell and Giuliani
- McGuireWoods Kazakhstan

Establishing a local company

Your very best bet as a newcomer to Kazakhstan is probably to find yourself a good agent (or a legal firm), but also to use the World Bank's very precise and detailed recipe for how to start a business in Kazakhstan. This way you can check that your representative is on the right track. This is what the World Bank's experts in Kazakhstan say you have to do to establish a business anywhere in Kazakhstan in 2009.

The Bank reckons that it takes a minimum of 21 days for a foreigner to establish a company in Kazakhstan, and a minimum of 8 different steps. This is not bad compared with Tajikistan (should you wish to establish there) where it takes 49 days, but worse than Uzbekistan or Kyrgyzstan where it only needs 15 days. Here (in brief) is how you go about it:

- **Notarise your Company Deed**
  You need to prepare your company deed in Kazakh and Russian (someone will have to translate it). You have to submit three copies to the Ministry of Justice and one to your notary. Then six sets of a Foundation Agreement have to be prepared, also in Kazakh and Russian, and one set given to each founder and one to your notary. It is reckoned that this can be done in one working day. Of course, preparation and translation of the documents have to be added to this.

- **Open a bank account, pay in the initial capital and pay the Ministry of Justice the registration fee**
  Here you have to open a local bank account in Kazakhstan and then pay in at least 25% of the charter capital and get a receipt for it before you register the company with the Ministry of Justice. You then have one year within which to pay in the remaining share capital. This procedure should be possible to complete within one working day.

- **State registration of the legal entity, statistical and tax registration with the local department of the Ministry of Justice**

  This is a relatively lengthy procedure, involving the registration of the company as a legal entity with the Ministry of Justice, the registration of the company in the State Statistical Register and the issue of a Tax Identification Number (TIN) and a taxpayer's certificate. These various procedures (which do require the submission of a considerable amount of paperwork from the company's side) are reckoned to take about fourteen days and the charge for a small business entity is KT2,280 or about US$150.

- **Register the company with the local tax office**

  Within ten days of registering the company with the Ministry of Justice, you have to register with your local tax office, and for income tax, social tax and Value Added Tax (VAT). This should not take more than one working day to do.

- **Make a company seal**

  This means registering a company seal by lodging a copy of the company registration, a power of attorney, a statistics card and a tax registration certificate together with a letter of application. This will take one working day, and can cost up to US$300.

- **Notarise the company registration and other post-registration documents**

  You will usually need a copy of the notarised documents to open a bank account, and another copy to register with the local tax office. Other notarised copies will be needed to get work permits to employ expatriates and for other activities. This will take one working day.

- **Open a current account for the company in the bank**

  To do this you need to produce sample signatures with the company seal, a copy of your tax registration, a copy of your company registration, a copy of your statistical registration, a notarised

7

copy of your company charter, copies of identity documents for the account signatories and the application form seeking to open an account. This process should take one working day.

• **Registration of compulsory life and health insurance for employees**
By law all employers must arrange for appropriate life and health insurance for all employees within ten days of the registration of the company. This process in itself should not take more than one working day.

Special economic zones

For investors with special interests, Kazakhstan has established four so-called 'Special Economic Zones' (SEZs). These are in Astana, on the left bank of the Ishim River (to encourage development), in Aktau on the Caspian Sea (to encourage the development of Aktau Sea Port), in Almaty (to encourage the development of the Information Technology Park) and on the 'Ontustik', industrial development park, which is a special economic zone near Shymkent in South Kazakhstan Oblast devoted to manufacturing. All of these zones offer special, tailor-made tax concessions to foreign investors.

Paying taxes

Kazakhstan has a well developed tax regime. All entities operating in Kazakhstan must register with the tax authorities. Corporate tax rates are 20% and personal income tax is charged at 10%. Value Added Tax (VAT) is chargeable at 12%. A company is obliged to register for VAT if its turnover exceeds USD 130,000 per annum – but a company can register for VAT voluntarily too. Needless to say it is smart to get yourself a proper adviser before getting too involved with the tax authorities.

Employing staff

Work permits are not required for foreign nationals who are on business trips not exceeding 60 days a year. They, of course, will still need one of the various visa types described in chapter 3, and to register with the immigration authorities where required. The Kazakhstan government has shown itself to be very sensitive to the issue of work permits for foreign nationals in the past, and has had run-ins with the oil and gas companies on a number of occasions. For example, there has been considerable resentment against companies bringing in catering staff and other service personnel who may well be experienced in their fields, but whose positions the government thinks Kazakhstanis could fill.

Work Permits

In applying for a work permit the employer has first to advertise locally for the position and satisfy the local labour office that no Kazakh candidates are available for the post. Then the employer has to apply for a work permit with the contract, a certified copy of educational documents, details of the candidate's work experience and a declaration that the candidate will leave Kazakhstan on completion of his/her contract. It can take two months or even more to get a work permit approved. The application for the work permit has to go to the local Regional Governor (the akim of the oblast) who determines the application.

7

Employing local staff is less complicated, but the Kazakhstan Labour Code of 15 May 2007 governs all employment contracts and the Ministry of Labour and Social Protection makes sure employers observe it.

Employing local staff

National employees should receive a contract specifying terms and condition, duties, working hours, remuneration, vacations – all of which, of course, have to be in conformity with the Labour Code. Minimum notice is one month. The working week is 40 hours. Employees are entitled to a minimum annual leave of 24 days, to sick leave and to maternity leave (126 days antenatal and post-natal). In fact, the Labour Code sets out conditions very similar to those prevailing in Europe and the United States. From September 2008 the monthly minimum wage in Kazakhstan was set at 13,183 *tenge* or US$88.

Labour Code

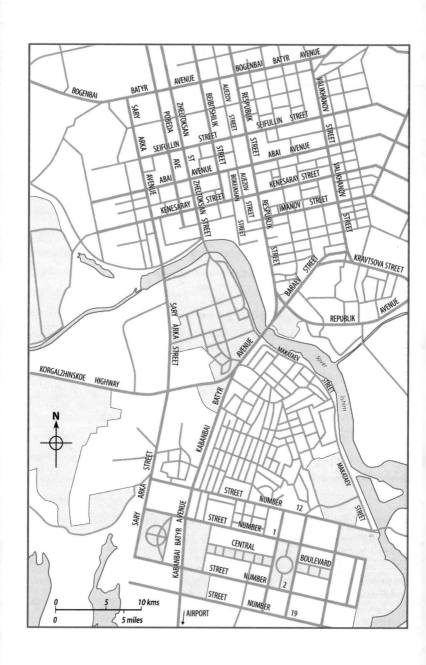

Detailed street maps are available in all major hotels

Astana

8

Astana

8 Astana

The nation's capital

Why Astana?

Astana has been Kazakhstan's capital for just over
ten years. Many countries have moved their capital cities
in the past one hundred years. But new capital cities have
met with varying degrees of success. Think of Canberra
in Australia, Brasilia in Brazil, Belmopan in Belize,
Yammousoukro in Cote d'Ivoire, Lilongwe in Malawi
and Dodoma in Tanzania. Plenty of countries have tried
it. Kazakhstan is one of them, having moved its capital
in 1997 from Almaty to Astana, and if it has not been a
success, it has certainly not been for the lack of trying.

Astana – then known as Akmola (or 'holy place') – was
designated as the new capital of Kazakhstan on 6 July
1994. Then it was an insignificant, provincial market town
of 200,000 folk, serving what remained of the 'Virgin
Lands' cereal-growing areas of northern Kazakhstan,
initiated by Khrushchev in the 1950s and 1960s. It was
to replace the former capital, and largest city, Alma-ata
(now known as Almaty). The capital actually moved from
Almaty on 10 December 1997 and was then renamed
(appropriately enough, but not very imaginatively)
Astana, which means 'capital city' in Kazakh.

8

The proposed move was met with considerable
scepticism, not least from the entrenched elites in
Almaty. Even the far-off *The Economist* magazine in
London was very sniffy about the whole idea, describing
the then Akmola as '...a drab Soviet-built town in the
windswept north of the country'. Many commentators
did not think it was a good idea to site a capital in a part
of the country submerged each year in a five-month
Siberian winter. However, Astana is on more or less
the same latitude as inland, but highly civilised and
sophisticated, cities like Calgary, Edmonton and Winnipeg
in Canada, and has no problem coping with blowing
snow and temperatures below -20 degrees Celsius.

Of course there were many sound reasons for moving the
capital from Almaty to Akmola/Astana. And when you
think about it, it was a very logical move indeed.

In 1994 Kazakhstan had been free of the Soviet Union
(and Russia) for less than three years. It still felt very like
Russia. In fact, because of the great, flat steppes in the

north of Kazakhstan, the country was more or less indistinguishable from the country over the border in southern Siberia, and felt very much like being back in Russia. Cities like Omsk and Chelyabinsk, just a few miles over the border in Russia were almost identical to Akmola and Kostanay on the Kazakh side. At the same time Kazakhstan's then capital Almaty lay almost one thousand miles to the south, perched in the south-east corner of Kazakhstan. It was a Central Asian city closer to China, India, Pakistan and Afghanistan than to the rest of the country.

But paradoxically too, although Almaty was a Central Asian city it also had a distinct Russian feel about it. It was here that the business and cultural life of the country revolved. Where the intellectuals and the business elite foregathered. It had been the capital and centre of things for so long that if you wanted to get anywhere in Kazakhstan you had to go to Almaty. There was nowhere else.

8

Reasons behind Nazarbayev's decision

As the savvy geopolitician that he was, President Nazarbayev saw that something had to be done. It was said that the Russian government was already eyeing large chunks of resource-rich northern Kazakhstan as a natural southwards extension of Siberia. Shifting the country's centre of gravity was the only option open to Kazakhstan for combating this. Moving the capital to a more northerly location, nearer the border with Russia, with a location more central and more accessible to the rest of the country was therefore a smart move. Most of northern Kazakhstan was inhabited by Russian speakers, and moving the capital to the north reinforced the north's Kazakh identity. Of course, President Nazarbayev also saw that a new capital was needed as a counterweight to Almaty and that the country was far too dependent on one city and one city alone.

But fear of Russian expansionism was not the only reason for moving the capital to Akmola/Astana. The President also had a new, growing and impatient Kazakh nation on his hands. Russian, German and other ethnic minorities were abandoning the country in a slow but steady trickle, preferring to return to their homelands. At the same time the Kazakhs, a people of the steppes, had nowhere else to go, and their numbers were increasing. As a largely rural people what they really needed was a new urban focus. Almaty was fine, but it was over 3,000 kilometres from the west of the country. It was still a large Russian provincial capital, and to get ahead you had to be a Russian speaker and part of the pan-Russian culture. Not really the place for an ambitious Kazakh speaker wanting to make headway in the new national Civil Service.

Another reason put forward for moving to Astana was the fear of earthquakes – to which Almaty was prone, being in the shadow of the Tian Shan Mountains. However, the real reason seems to have been a geopolitical one. Kazakhstan needed a national focus for an emerging and self-confident Kazakh nation. A capital that was more easily accessible from the rest of the country and which would re-establish Kazakh sovereignty over the north of the country – in other words, a capital that the Kazakhs could call their own.

8

History

The present settlement of Akmola or Akmolinsk on which Astana is based started life as a military fort established by the Cossacks in 1824 on the Ishim River. However, recent archaeological research has shown that there has been a Kazakh military and commercial presence at Bozok in the vicinity of the present-day Astana for over one thousand years (based on Silk Road trading). During the nineteenth century a town grew up slowly on the basis of the railway. In the 1930s one of Stalin's notorious Gulags was established about 30 kms to the south-west of the city (you can still see remains of it today). In 1961 the town was renamed Tselinograd or 'Virgin Lands City' and became the capital of the Virgin Lands. These were 330,000 km^2 (an area bigger than the United Kingdom) of flat, prairie-land or steppe, designated for cereal production by Khrushchev. Over 300,000 immigrants, mainly Russians, but also many Germans flocked to the area, and this is why there are still relatively few Kazakh speakers today in northern Kazakhstan. At independence in 1991 the town reverted to its original Kazakh name of Akmola.

Akmola

Tselinograd

8

Planning and design in Astana

Since its designation in 1994 Astana has become a happy hunting ground for architects and city planners. In 1998 the government held an international competition for a master plan and design of the new city of Astana, attracting over fifty international architect firms. The competition was won by the Japanese architect/planner **Kisho Kurokawa**. He planned a city for the twenty-first century expanding the city population from 300,000 to 600,000 by 2005 and to one million by 2030. Kurokawa planned to preserve and redevelop the existing city on the north side of the Ishim River while developing a new business and government city on the south side of the river towards the new airport. Much of Kurokawa's plans have been followed and Kurokawa was also responsible for the design of the brand new Astana Airport. Kisho Kurokawa lived to see much of his vision implemented and died in 2007. Most of his plans were implemented by the city's chief planner Vladimir Laptev.

The city plan has been followed by an amazing succession of individual buildings all of which are dovetailed into the plan. From an architectural point of view there is certainly nowhere else like Astana on the planet! The new city quarter on the left bank (south side) of the Ishim River is a splendid mixture of mock Islamic/oriental, neo-Soviet and post-modern architectural styles, topped off by some stunning individual buildings. The first new buildings tended to a 'kitsch' style based on a quasi-mythical orientalism, with shiny domes and bounding arches, sometimes shoddily built. But standards have improved and internationally renowned architects have turned up producing some really spectacular pieces of architecture in a flat steppe landscape where you would certainly not expect to see it. Architecturally it is safe to say that Astana is something else! Astana is certainly built on the grand scale, and is built for the car and the taxi and not for the cyclist or the pedestrian.

Astana is proud of its 'Bayterek' or observation tower which soars to over 100 metres on the left bank area. It was one of the first buildings completed there in 2003. An observation tower is a good idea in a country as flat as that round Astana. The tower symbolises a poplar tree in which the mythical Samruk bird has laid its egg. It is

Kisho Kurokawa

Architecture

Bayterek

Astana's most recognizable symbol, and eager groups of Kazakh tourists photograph each other at its base – to show the folks back home. On the observation platform on the top you can view the emerging city, and in a golden handprint of President Nazarbayev, you can insert your own hand – and make a wish, as the guide will urge you.

But there are a number of other striking buildings – there is always something new every time you return to Astana's emerging Left Bank. The Ak Orda (meaning white horde) is the President's new office, built in 2004. It is 80 metres high and topped by the blue dome which seems to characterise many of Kazakhstan's newer official buildings – maybe to give it a whiff of Central Asia. The British celebrity architect Sir Norman Foster (whose firm designed Beijing Airport, the biggest building on the planet) designed the Palace of Peace and Reconciliation (the so-called 'Pyramid of Peace') in 2006. The concept is to serve as a meeting place for the world religions – hopefully every three years. It also contains the Natural History Museum and a 1,500 seat Opera House. As is becoming usual in Astana, the Pyramid is huge and is 77 metres high. Foster has also designed one of the world's most spectacular and ambitious constructions, the Khan Shatyry Entertainment Centre (http://www.khanshatyry.com). This is a giant tent structure, 150 metres high, which will house apartments, shopping, entertainment complexes, football fields and botanic gardens. Khan Shatyry, which was still under construction in mid 2009, seems to set out to rival some of the wilder extravagances of Dubai. In 2007-2008 the top Italian architects, Manfredi and Luca Nicoletti designed a stunning new State Auditorium, one of the largest auditoria in the world, designed to seat over 3,500 people. It too is under construction.

But if Astana has been an interesting challenge for many world architects, it has been a godsend for the Turkish construction industry. Much of Astana has been built by Turkish contractors who have flocked to the city since its inauguration as capital in 1997. The Turkish and Kazakh languages are said to be mutually intelligible. Thus Turkish speakers have a great advantage in Kazakhstan, an advantage they have grasped with two

8

Pyramid of Peace

Khan Shatyry Entertainment Centre

Turkish contruction industry

hands, as Turkish exporters and contractors in Astana have boomed over the past ten years.

With all of this new construction Astana has almost grown out of recognition over the past ten years. The old city on the right bank of the Ishim has been refurbished and a glistening new city has emerged on the left bank. In 1997 the population was about 250,000 and now it is nearing 700,000. Less than ten years ago there was one international flight connection to Astana – from Moscow. Now Astana has direct connections from its spanking new international airport to Abu Dhabi, Amsterdam, Antalya, Dubai, Frankfurt, Istanbul, Kaliningrad, Kiev, Moscow, St Petersburg, Sharjah, Urumchi and Vienna.

With all the newness around it is very easy to be bedazzled by Astana, especially when you drive in from the airport to be confronted by towering new government office buildings, one of the world's largest mosques (financed by the Emir of Qatar), shopping malls, the Presidential offices, an Oceanarium (on former steppe land) or soaring new bridges over the sluggish old Ishim River.

The ethnic mix

With so much newness around it is tempting to overlook the old Astana (or Akmola) which, of course, has been there upon the right bank of the Ishim for over one hundred years. In misguided efforts to create a new symbol for the independent Kazakhstan, some government people have been over-eager to pull down the lovely nineteenth-century wooden dachas, with their sprawling vegetable gardens that characterised the old Astana.

Old Astana

It is thus easy to dismiss the old town as a dismal relic of the Soviet command economy. However, beneath the surface there is an interesting ethnic mix not immediately apparent to the casual, non-Russian speaking business visitor in a hurry to get his work over, and to get on to his plane home. During the 1930s and 1940s Stalin had a tendency to banish troublesome ethnic minorities, especially from the Caucasus, but also from the rest of the Soviet Union, to northern Kazakhstan where the opportunities for political mischief were very limited. Thus Astana has a fair sprinkling of ethnic Chechens,

8

Ingush and Tartars who still maintain their languages and culture, and you will often come upon a troupe of Chechen girls entertaining at a school concert with their colourful dances. Stalin also set up a series of 'Gulag' concentration camps south of Astana close to the iron and coal mines of Karaganda where troublemakers from all over the Soviet Union were gathered. Not all of those who managed to survive the hellish conditions chose to return to their original homelands in Belarus, Ukraine, Russia or the Baltics. Often it was too far to go home or they had been forgotten by their families or they had established new-found families here in Kazakhstan. Thus many former Gulag inmates made their homes in and around Astana. Then during the 1950s and 1960s over 300,000 optimistic souls made their way eastwards from Russia, Ukraine, Belarus and the Volga German area to serve as Young Pioneers in the Virgin Lands. They settled around Astana and many never went home.

8

However, since Astana became the capital, the ethnic mix has changed considerably as there has been a great influx of young Kazakh families. These have supplanted the older Slav residents of Astana. This latter group began to see their days in Kazakhstan as numbered. They had a poorer (usually technical) education than the Kazakhs and they did not speak Kazakh (and were not interested in learning it either). Without being able to speak Kazakh they had no chance of finding work in the growing Civil Service (except in menial posts like drivers or mechanics). Interestingly enough, ethnic Kazakhs from the north of Kazakhstan who do not speak Kazakh are also excluded from most government service jobs. Thus discrimination is on linguistic grounds and not on the basis of ethnicity.

Influx of young Kazakh families

The foreigner in Astana

There is no getting away from it. Of all capitals in the world, for a Western businessperson, Astana is one of the most 'foreign' you can visit. Particularly in the depths of a Siberian winter. On a superficial level, Western ways have penetrated the city with shopping malls, glittering restaurants, swish hotels and towering office blocks. But at street level you often feel yourself back in the good old USSR. Street signs and street maps are all in the Russian language (and Cyrillic script). Your spoken Russian has to be good if you are going to get a response out of a passer-by, especially an older one. The only folk who will volunteer any English at all (apart from hotel staff), are giggling teenagers who may be able to string a few words together, but not much more. Few restaurants outside the big hotels will offer a menu in anything but Russian, although waiters are helpful enough in trying to explain to you what you are ordering. Even in some of the poshest restaurants, addressing the maître d' in anything but Russian can be met with a blank stare. And try finding a copy of *Time* or *Newsweek*. Good luck. They do exist but are not easy to track down. There can't be many Irish pubs in the world where you have to order your pint of Guinness in Russian or travel agencies where you have to rebook your flight to Frankfurt where no one speaks English or German.

Of course the city is changing as more embassies and more international organisations move in. But these too are usually self-sufficient and their international staff do not have to go out in the town so much. They are there to interact with each other and the government and not the people. Astana is still a city for government people and not businessfolk. Most businesspeople will visit Astana for a day or two at the most – for a meeting with the Ministry – but will soon return to the more business-friendly atmosphere of Almaty.

Hotels – the Top End
Okan InterContinental Astana
113 Abaya Avenue, Astana, Kazakhstan
Tel: +7 7172 391000
Email: www.ichotelsgroup.com

It is not easy to imagine how it was to be a visiting businessman in Astana before 10 June 1998. On that date the splendid Turkish financed and owned Okan Intercontinental opened. Before that, the choice was limited to a series of spartan, Soviet-inspired establishments with brick-hard mattresses and surly concierges.

Getting the chairman of the Okan Holding Group Bekir Okan to build and run this world-class hotel in the new capital, was an inspirational move by President Nazarbayev. Without it, Astana would have struggled to attract foreign institutions or diplomatic visitors to give the city legitimacy. In the early days, international oil companies and financial institutions took offices in the hotel, and the few shivering foreign visitors could be assured a warm welcome from the biting, snow-filled blasts off the steppe, recharging their batteries on Italian coffee and malt whisky.

Now, more than ten years on, Astana has a plethora of fine business hotels to complement the Okan Intercontinental, which is now one of the three five-star hotels in the city. The others are:

8

The Rixos President Hotel
Astana City Centre, Astana
Tel: +7 7172 245050
Email: astana@rixos.com
Website: http://www.rixos.com/astana/

This is a very plush 168-bedroom hotel, opened in 2005 on the left bank in the middle of the government district. It is part of the Turkish Rixos hotel chain which has also opened in Almaty. It appears to have the only good English bookshop in Astana, with a wide range of books and magazines on Kazakhstan, as well as lots of foreign-language magazines and newspapers.

The Radisson SAS Hotel
Sary Arka 4, Astana 010000
Tel: +7 7172 990000
Email: info.astana@radissonsas.com
Website: http://www.radissonsas.com

This is situated right on the bank of the Ishim River (on the right bank). It was voted the 'Leading Hotel in Kazakhstan' in the World Travel Awards for 2008, and has all the facilities expected of a world-class business hotel, i.e. presidential suites, Italian restaurant and wellness and fitness centre.

It is difficult to generalise about room rates as many different deals are available on the Internet. However, five-star luxury in Astana does not come cheap and room rates can range from US$350 to US$600 or more.

Some Other Hotels

Now there is no shortage of good hotels in Astana and it is very easy to locate and book the sort of hotel you are looking for on http://www.astana-hotels.net Here you can find yourself a room from US$47 and up. Here is an idiosyncratic selection of three reasonable hotels in Astana:

The Hotel Grand Park Esil
8 Beibitshilik, Astana 010000
Tel: +7 7172 591901
Email: reservaions@grandparkesil.kz
Website: http://www.grandparkesil.kz

This is the old Ishim Hotel which, at one time, must have been the classical (and only) Soviet Intourist hotel of the old Akmola. It is a wonderfully classical pile, bristling with columns, pillars and balustrades from the 1920s and is bang in the centre of the older part of the city. It was completely (thank God!) refurbished in 2004. It has 132 rooms and a useful Health Club. The rates are around US$150 a night.

Imperia G Hotel
Abay Street 63, Astana 010000
Tel: +7 7172 405501

The Imperia G is in a new block close to the old centre and handy for the shops. It is quiet, has all the services, an English-speaking reception and a business centre. It comes out about US$120 a night.

Altyn Dala
Pionerskaya 19A,
Astana 010000
Tel: +7 7172 323311
Email: altyn-dala@mail.kz

This is a small intimate hotel with 76 rooms, perched just behind the Ministry of Finance in the old town. It is well

known amongst foreign business visitors for being clean
and reasonable so it is wise to book up early.

Restaurants

No restaurant is Astana is much more than ten years old.
At the same time, the city has had to get its act together
pretty quickly indeed, and to prepare itself for an influx
of Ministers, top politicians, civil servants, diplomats
and, not least, visiting dignitaries from all over the world
coming to pay court to the capital of this oil-rich new
Central Asian nation – and all of them expect to eat well.

Astana has risen admirably to the challenge and built a
bewildering range of eateries. The result is an eclectic
mix of Argentinian, Azeri, British, Central Asian, Dutch,
French, Georgian, German, Italian, Jamaican, Japanese,
Swedish and Ukrainian cuisine. One of the strangest
sights in the new Astana is Sary Arka Avenue on the left
bank where a series of country-themed restaurants have
been built. At the last count there were a Central Asian,
a Japanese, a Korean, a Swedish, an Arabian and a Dutch
restaurant. Predictably the Dutch restaurant is announced
by a huge windmill and the Central Asian one by a blue-
tiled dome. It can also be a trifle disconcerting in the Tre
Kronor Swedish Beer House to be confronted by a
Kazakh waiter rigged out in Swedish national dress.

If your assignment in Astana takes you into power-lunch
country, then you cannot go far wrong in the posh
restaurants of the Intercontinental (the Eurasia Grill),
the Radisson SAS (the French Brasserie Capri) or the
President Hotel.

Otherwise the following are worth investigating:

Astana Nur, 3/2 Respublik Avenue which has a fine
terrace on the river Ishim, and makes the most of it in
summer. It does both European food and specialities
from the Caucasus Region. Tel: +7 7172 223922.

Chelsea English Pub, 7 Respublik Avenue. Unlikely
looking football-themed pub, but does good solid
European meals and beer. Tel: +7 7172 217727

8

Derby Bar & Grill, 8 Irchenko Street is more or less next door to the Radisson SAS and attracts a cosmopolitan crowd with its European and Japanese cuisine.

East-West, 2/2 Kabanbai Batyr Avenue, Egorkino, 93 Auezov Street, AREA, does Indian, Kazakh and Italian menus and the restaurant is divided into these sections. Tel: +7 7172 243054

Egorkino, 93 Auezov Street. Mainly Russian cuisine and the restaurant is well established, having been in Astana ten years. Tel: +7 7172 323878

Farhi, 3 Bokeikhan Street (just off Kenesary), AREA. This is one of Astana's first traditional Kazakh restaurants where you can sample all the traditional Kazakh dishes. Tel: +7 7172 321899

Izymi, 32 Kabanbai Batyr Avenue, Kruglaya Ploshad. This is a small and quite exclusive Japanese restaurant. Tel: +7 7172 242723

Korolevskaya Ohota, Near the Eurasia 2 Trade Centre, Microdistrict 4. This is one of Astana's poshest restaurants doing regal delicacies like wild boar and venison. Tel: +7 7172 341817

La Riviere, 2 Kabanbai Batyr Avenue, AREA. As the name implies this is a classy, and quite pricey, French restaurant down by the River Ishim. Tel: +7 7172 242260

Line Brew, 20 Kenesary Street, AREA. This is done as a medieval castle and is basically a grill/steakhouse. Its speciality is local steaks and shashlyk.
Tel: +7 7172 236373

Mori, Avenue, AREA. This is another minimalistic Japanese cuisine place, not far from the Radisson.
Tel: +7 7172 241024

North Wind English Pub, 12 Samal Building. One of the earliest attempts at recreating the English pub in Astana. Classy menu and live music at night.
Tel: +7 7172 223346

8

Pivovaroff, 24 Beibitshilik Street, AREA. This is a German restaurant specialising in German delicacies, and also brewing its own beer. Tel: +7 7172 328866

Satti, 32 Kabanbai Batyr Avenue, Kruglaya Ploshad. Here the food is mainly European and Kazakh and they provide music and dancing. Tel: +7 7172 242848

Tiflis, 14 Imanov Street (between Respublik and Valikhanov), AREA. This, of course, is one of Astana's best Georgian restaurants with lots of Georgian favourites and wines. Tel: +7 7172 221226

Tre Kronor, 17 Sary Arka Avenue, AREA. This is an unlikely-looking Swedish-themed beerhouse on the left bank, but with good food and beer.
Tel: +7 7172 402025

Vaquero, 5 Beibitshilik Street (just off Kenesary), AREA, is notionally a Latin American restaurant with Argentinan and Mexican dishes, but also does European.
Tel: +7 7172 390121

Venezia, 9 Beibitshilik Street, 1st Floor, Sine Tempore Shopping Mall, AREA. Well-established and well-liked Italian restaurant on the right bank.
Tel: +7 7172 753906

Yamayka, 51 Abai Street. Well-established Jamaican restaurant but diversified now. Good live music at night.
Tel: +7 7172 323569

Zhibek Zholy, 102 Abai Avenue (Valikhanov), AREA. Named the 'Silk Road' in Kazakh, this does Central Asian and Chinese food and is a mixture of styles.
Tel: +7 7172 210507

What to do on a rainy/snowy day?

At first sight Astana can be a pretty soulless spot, especially if you are there over a weekend with not much to do. This is even more so in the dead of winter when the city often feels sealed off from the rest of the world by great snowfalls. True, your hotel will certainly have wireless Internet and any number of TV channels. But

8

then who wants to sit and watch TV all day? That, you can do at home.

Local Kazakh or Russian residents in Astana have no real tradition of entertaining at home, so unless you are lucky, you are not likely to be invited home to someone's place for dinner. Although as we show above there is no shortage of pubs and restaurants in which to while away the time.

But in Astana, if you show a bit of initiative and have a bit of luck, you can fall back on the two great pastimes of culture and sport. There is a lot of both in Astana but finding out what is going on needs some perseverance. At one time there was a Vienna-based publication called *What's on in Astana* (http://www.whatsonastana.com) but that seems to have died a death early in 2008 and has not made a reappearance since. The major hotels should provide a briefing on what is going on in town, but do not seem to have got round to it yet.

National Academy of Music

On the cultural side, one positive legacy of the Soviet Union has been the opera, ballet and classical music which you can enjoy in Astana. Kazakhs and Russians alike are great lovers of classical music and ballet and are eager practitioners as well. You can attend Western and Kazakh classical music concerts at the Kazakh National Academy of Music at 65 Pobeda Avenue (Tel: +7 7172 239294: http://www.kaznam.kz). Here you can also see Kazakh folk music and singing. The Academy was founded in 1998 and is thriving as never before. For opera and ballet you would go to the K.Bajseitova National Opera and Ballet Theatre on Akzhayk Street (Tel: +7 7172 392761). Here you can see Western classics like *Eugene Onegin* or *Coppelia* or the more exotic Kazakh national ballet. The huge Congress Hall at Kenesary Street 32 (Tel: +7 7172 752383) on the right bank is a well-established venue with symphony concerts, ballet, pop concerts and folk dance. The venerable Gorky Russian Drama Theatre at Zheltoksan St. 11 (Tel: +7 7172 328223) puts on popular and classic theatre, but you are not going to get much out of it unless your Russian is fluent. Perhaps more accessible is the Astana Circus, now housed in a circular, flying saucer shaped

National Opera and Ballet Theatre

building on the left bank of the city. As in almost all post-Soviet societies, the circus is very popular in Kazakhstan and the Astana Circus, with its 2,000 seats is no exception. It is on Kurgaldzhinoskoe highway 2/1 (Tel: +7 7172244059)

And with the vast new State Auditorium being built on the left bank, culture vultures in Astana can expect a lot more for their money in the coming years.

Football

Spectator sport is only now taking off in Astana, but there is already a lot to see. Astana has always had top football, but has now built up a new Premier league team called FC Lokomotiv Astana playing at the Kazimukhan Munaitpasov Stadium. You can see FC Lokomotiv play every second week in the summer between April and September. They were very successful in 2009, partly due to their ability to import foreign players, mainly from Russia.

8

Ice hockey

In winter if live sport is your thing, you should certainly try to see Barys ('Snow Leopard') of Astana who play in the new Kontinental Ice Hockey League which consists of 24 professional ice hockey teams from Russia, Kazakhstan, Latvia and Belarus. The atmosphere at the Alatau Sports Palace with 5,500 spectators urging on Barys against a Russian rival team is hard to beat. Players are recruited from all over the world and the current captain is Canadian Kevin Dallman.

Basketball

Nor is any new city worth its salt without its own basketball team. The Astana Tigers now play in the Kazakhstan National Basketball League, and have built up a keen following in the city.

Cycling

For a vast number of sports fans, Astana is known for one thing and one thing only, and that is the Astana Cycling team. This is an international team of professional cyclists recruited from US (Lance Armstrong), Spain, Germany, Slovenia, Portugal, Switzerland, Lithuania, and, of course, Kazakhstan. The team is sponsored by a number of major Kazakh industries, e.g. KazMunaiGas, Air Astana, ENRC and Temir Zholy. However, your chances of seeing Team Astana in Astana itself are pretty remote. They had no scheduled appearances whatsoever in Kazakhstan in the first half of 2009.

The possibilities of participating in sport yourself in Astana are pretty limited, but not non-existent.

In winter you can hire skates and go skating at the Kazakhstan Sports Centre at 9 Munaitpasov Street and you can even go cross-country skiing (if you can locate a pair of skis) on the frozen Ishim River where tracks are laid out. You could also try your hand at ice-fishing, that is fishing through a hole in the ice on the Ishim River, which is a very popular sport with the locals. Also in winter Astana organises the construction of an 'Ice Town' on the banks of the Ishim River where a large variety of ice structures are built.

There are several other attractions worth visiting in Astana. One is the lovely painted Cathedral Church of the Holy Constantine and Helena visited day and night by crowds of Orthodox believers. It was erected in 1900, and is approached past a long line of supplicant beggars, so one is well advised to carry a large pocketful of small coins. It is located jut off Respublika Avenue. Another more earthy spot is Astana's central market which was moved to the right bank to an area called Shankhai (or Shanghai) which indicates that most of the goods are of Chinese provenance (mainly clothes). This is on Sofievskaya trassa on the east side of town on the route out to Pavlodar. It is seething with life, with exotic ethnic groups, Uzbeks selling figs and currants, Belorussians selling fur hats and Chinese selling fake Omega watches at a dollar a time – they can last anything from ten minutes up to a year. Unlike the church, the market is somewhere you do not display your money – the pick-pocketing is notorious.

Finally as a curiosity. Astana's new Oceanarium at the Duman Centre on the left bank is worth a mention. If only because of its boast for being the only Oceanarium more than 3,000 kilometres from the sea! They say they needed over 120 tonnes of sea salt to get it right. It is rather unreal to watch sharks, giant rays, Amazonian piranhas and delicate coral fish on the steppes of central Asia.

9

other major cities

other major cities

Whatever else he does, the business traveller visiting Kazakhstan will not be going there for its cities. Because of its huge size, Kazakhstan is not noted for its cities or for its city life. In fact, Kazakhstan is actually an awful lot of empty steppe with its cities far from each other.

The cities themselves are relatively small – only Almaty has more than one million inhabitants – and they are a long way apart. The distance between the first and second cities, i.e. Astana and Almaty is 1,250 kms by road (like driving from London to Nice on the French Riviera), and from Almaty to the new oil capital, Atyrau on the Caspian Sea, it is 2,700 kms (like driving from London to northern Greece). Driving around Kazakhstan can be a lonely affair, with few places to stop off and not a lot to see, but, strangely enough, there are also a number of fair-sized cities with between a quarter of a million and a half a million people each. These were often due to the Soviet central planning system. During the 1930s and 1940s the Soviet Union began to realise what huge mineral riches Kazakhstan was sitting on, and so built up a series of sizeable cities designed to exploit these minerals. As the area was so vast, and there were so few people around, they could afford to pollute as much as they liked. Nor did it matter if there was no fresh-water there on the spot, as the authorities simply pumped and piped water for hundreds of kilometres to where it was needed. In other countries people migrate from the smaller cities to the big ones, to get a better life. In Kazakhstan people were often simply planted in a city, and told to get on with it. Thus the visiting businessman may just as likely end up in a large provincial city like Karaganda or Shymkent as Astana or Almaty. This chapter thus gives a brief overview of no fewer than 13 different cities outside the capital, Astana.

9

In 2009 about half of Kazakhstan's population of 16 million lived in cities. In fact, most of Kazakhstan's cities are a product of the Soviet era. And the Soviet influence shows. There is a dispiriting sameness about the monolithic public buildings, squares, parks and statuary, and the monotonous prefabricated, industrialised housing blocks, pushed up in a hurry to house industrial workers, do not make for attractive cities. Kazakhstan is also still struggling to clear up the Soviet legacy of industrial pollution in its cities.

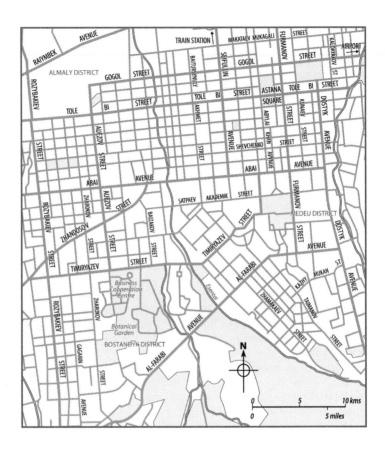

Almaty

But there are, of course, exceptions. The leafy, tree-lined boulevards of Almaty, with their laid-back cafes and bars, the pleasant walks along the Syr Darya river in Kyzylorda, the startling, sky-blue mosque in Kostanay, the charming Tsarist public buildings of Uralsk. These are some of the bright spots. A few towns, of course, are largely new like Astana or Atyrau, but the Soviet period was not kind to Kazakhstan as a whole. It left behind a run-down infrastructure, poor hotels, few good restaurants, ubiquitous power lines and an awful lot of idle, heavy industry blotting the landscape. So, contain your disappointment.

Almaty

It is, therefore, as well to start with Kazakhstan's most attractive city. It is also the largest, the oldest and the best established. In almost every one of the Soviet Union's 16 republics, there was one capital city where the power brokers and the intelligentsia, the artists and the politicians foregathered. In the Ukraine it was in Kiev, in Latvia it was Riga and in Kazakhstan it was Alma-Ata, which is how Almaty was known until 1993. It is here that you will meet many of Kazakhstan's most switched on folk.

It is difficult for the casual visitor to say whether Almaty is a Central Asian city or a Russian one. The throbbing Zelyony 'Green' market in the city centre and the huge Barakholkha general market on the outskirts are certainly characterised by the noise, colour, movement and ambience you would associate with Central Asia. They are full of Uighurs, Dungans, Tajiks, Chinese, Kazakhs and Russians selling a bewildering array of fruit, herbs, nuts, vegetables and consumer imports from Russia, China and Turkey.

9

On the other hand, the city is spaciously laid out in a rectangular grid of pleasant squares and boulevards lined with towering white poplars and black, Central Asian elms (karagaches). This is a generous pre-Soviet Russian city, laid out after the terrible earthquake and landslides of 1911.

Nonetheless, despite its orderly and pleasing layout, Almaty can be quite confusing for the visitor. The reason is as follows. The city is bordered on at least two sides by the great Kazakh steppe stretching away to the north and west into a great emptiness. The city inclines at first gently, and then abruptly upwards to the south and east, eventually rising precipitately into the great Tian Shan Mountains bordering Kyrgyzstan. The visitor is then confronted with a city map where the Tian Shan Mountains are shown, to the south, at the bottom of the map, and the city tilts gently northwards (and downwards) up to the top of the map, and then on to the infinity of the great Kazakh steppe. Somehow the first-time visitor feels the land should tilt up the map towards the top rather than the other way round. Almaty feels a bit topsy-turvy, but it is something you eventually do get used to.

Almaty has no real city centre in the true sense of the word, but it is none the worse for that. Instead it is intersected by a series of boulevards running east-west (Raimbeka Avenue, Gogol Street, Tole Bi Street, Shevchenko Street, Abai Avenue and Satpayev Street) and running north-south (Mukanov Street, Seyfullin Aenue, Furmanov Street and Dostyk Avenue), so that it is in fact very easy to find your way about. All you really need to do in Almaty is to orientate yourself by looking upwards and finding the towering, snow-capped Tian Shan range which forms the city's southern limits. Thereafter everything will fit into place. In any event your hotel will be on one part of the grid that makes up the city and you can soon find your way around by finding your nearest east-west and north-south streets.

9

Hound Dog Hole – Pre-9/11

The Cafe Hound Dog Hole in the US Embassy in Almaty was never any ordinary cafe. Its kitchen had originally belonged to Elvis Presley. On his military service in Germany in 1959 Elvis bought an entire kitchen for the unit he served with, and when he left he donated it to the US Army on the Rhine. In 1994 with the end of the Cold War, and the fall of the Berlin Wall, the kitchen was broken up. For some unknown reason a large chunk of it was bought for the US Embassy in Almaty and it was transported stock, lock and barrel to the Embassy on Aiteke Bi Street. When the word got round it became almost an object of pilgrimage for Elvis fans. At least until 11 September 2001, any ordinary person could use it, have a coffee, browse the newspapers and watch US TV. The only condition was that you deposited your passport with security at the entrance gate. The Scottish catering supervisor, Jim Oliver, was quoted as saying 'We are cooking with reverence!'

It is strange to think in these post 9/11 days that, not so long ago, you could stop off and meet your pals for your morning coffee in downtown Almaty, inside the American Embassy. Those were the days!

Certainly the most striking feature of Almaty for the first-time visitor is the proximity of the Tian Shan mountains. Or the Zailysky Alatau range as they are known locally. There is no city in the world where the Mountains rise more than 4,000 metres (12,000 feet) more or less from the city boundaries. In fact, the mountains are no more than a 30 minute bus or taxi ride from downtown Almaty (see the next chapter). The best time to see the mountains from Almaty is in the early morning or in the evening when you are not dazzled by the glare of the southern sun above the mountains themselves. And the best time of the year to see the city is in spring (April and May) when much of the more prosperous southern suburbs are covered in thick almond, apple, cherry and apricot blossom.

Tian Shan Mountains

Otherwise Almaty is a cultivated and sophisticated city, befitting its decades as the capital of the country and the centre of its business activity. It still has many embassies, although some of the bigger ones have moved to Astana, and it has retained most of the really big international businesses, financial and legal firms. It also has ambitious plans for development as a Central Asian financial hub, despite the hiccoughs being experienced with the ongoing financial crisis. The Regional Financial Centre for Almaty (RFCA) which, like many of Kazakhstan's institutions, is said to be a brainchild of President Nazarbayev. It got off the ground in 2006 and is said to have been inspired by the financial centres in Dubai, Ireland and Singapore. It incorporates the Kazakhstan Stock Exchange and a whole new complex of banks and financial offices is being constructed to the south of Republic Square on the south side of the city. In 2008 Lord Norman Foster designed twin 48-story towers for the financial centre of Almaty. Whether these ever actually get built in the present financial crisis remains to be seen.

9

Regional Financial Centre for Almaty

Getting Around in Almaty

Because of its mature trees and its pleasant boulevards (some of which are pedestrianised) Almaty can be a pleasant city to wander about in on foot, if you can cope with the relentless traffic and the crumbling pavements and sidewalks. Perhaps one should be careful at night, because, although the city is well lit, its wealth and sophistication also attract unsavoury elements from all over Central Asia, and taxis are so cheap it is not worth chancing it.

Maybe the best way of getting about for a business visitor is to hire a chauffeur-driven car by the hour or by the day. That will cost you anything from US$15 to US$35 an hour, depending on the standard of car. That way you

Chauffeurs and taxis

do not have the hassle of finding your way through the traffic or of finding a small office on the fourth floor in a backyard. There the driver should be able to find it for you. Otherwise you can use taxis by simply standing in the street and waving down what looks like a likely vehicle – there seem to be many more 'pirate' or freelance taxis than official ones in Almaty and they should cost about US$2 within Almaty centre. Embassies often warn visitors against doing this, but it should be OK in daylight at least. The trouble is you have to have a map and know more or less where you are heading. Otherwise your hotel can order you a radio cab.

9

Almaty also has a huge, rickety tramcar network, but that is only for those with unlimited time at their disposal

Tram

and not really practical for a business traveller. The city has also been building an underground Metro system over many years, but it has been plagued by shortages of funds and changes in policy. However the latest word is that the first 8 kilometres of a planned 45 kilometre network will open sometime in 2010.

Sleeping, eating, drinking and entertainment in Almaty

Not surprisingly, Almaty sports most of the best hotels in the country, several of which were built and/or are run by Turkish entrepreneurs. Space limits us to a few of the better known which are:

The Hyatt Regency
29/6 Satpayev Street

The Intercontinental Almaty
181 Zhetokhsan Street

Hotel Kazakhstan
52 Dostyk Street

Hotel Dostyk Residence
162 Furmanov Street

Astana International Hotel
113 Baitursynuly Street

Hotel Otrar
73 Gogol Street

The Holiday Inn, Almaty
2D Timiryazev Street

None of these is cheap, although you can probably get a single room at the Hotel Kazakhstan, for around US$130. This is Almaty's oldest business hotel, built for Intourist in the early 1970s, and has undergone a series of makeovers, some successful, some less so. The other hotels range from US$150 up to US$400 or more. In Almaty if you want to go under US$100 a night it may mean going to hotels which to take you '. . . *back to the USSR* . . .' with surly concierges, frightful breakfasts and call-girls prepared to ring your phone off the hook.

Prices

9

Two very superior hotels, the Almaty Marriott, situated in the classier southern suburbs, and the Radisson Blu, a resort hotel close to the Medeo Skating Rink in the foothills of the Tian Shan Mountains, are due to open in Almaty in 2010. They will greatly increase the high-quality accommodation available in the city.

Eating well in Almaty is not difficult, given the huge and ever-changing choice of restaurants. With the ethnic mix of Kazakhstan you can eat local Kazakh, Russian, German, Uighur, Tartar, Korean and Chechen cuisine at the very least, whilst American, French, Italian, Chinese and Thai have also made their inroads. Again, space limits us to naming some of the better-known and reputed eateries in Almaty:

Dastarkhan
75 Shevchenko Street
(Russian, Kazakh)

Venezia,
87 Dostyk Avenue
(Italian)
Tel: +7 727 2 640995

Princess Turandot,
103 Abai Avenue
(Chinese)

Korean House
Gogol street, 2
(Korean)
Tel: +7 727 2 939692

Beirut Restaurant,
Dostyk Ave. 50.
(Lebanese)
Tel: +7 727 2 938191

Alasha Restaurant,
Marat Ospanov Street, 20
(Uzbek)
Tel: +7 727 2 540700

Mad Murphy's Irish Pub
Tole Bi Street, 12.
(European/American)
Tel: +7 727 2 912856

Pirosmani
Abilai Khan Ave, 32.
(Georgian)
Tel: +7 727 2 392525

Entrecote Restaurant
1- Bogenbai Batyr Street,
(International)
Tel: +7 727 2 964415

An Almaty website calling itself the CIA (Club Intelligence Assessment) claims that there are a couple of dozen nightclubs and over forty casinos in Almaty. At least it is good to know that someone has counted. It is also reassuring to realise that, in a country which many Westerners believe is a Muslim one, you can drink and gamble the night away seven nights a week. By its very nature the nightclub and casino scene changes every week so that the best way to orient yourself is to check the latest reviews of which there are hundreds on the Internet.

There is not much to beat a summer's night under the towering poplars in an outdoor cafe or bar on Almaty's boulevards – and there is no shortage of cooling drinks. Kazakhstan produces the excellent Tian Shan, Alma-ata, Karaganda, Shhymkent and Derbes (Turkish) beers. You can also try Kazakh wines which are produced from vineyards round Almaty. Grape production started in the fifties and wine production was inspired by wine-makers from Georgia and Moldova. There are about four winemakers producing both red and white wines as well as a rather flamboyant 'champagne'.

Kazakh beer and wine

Nor is there any shortage of more formal entertainment in Almaty. You can see classical opera and ballet at the recently restored classical Abai Kazakh State Opera and Ballet Theatre at 110 Kabanbai Batyr Street. It puts on both classical Western opera and Kazakh opera. There is also no shortage of classical concerts at the Zhambyl Kazakh State Philharmonia (every two or three nights) on Tole Bi and at the Kazakh Concert Hall on Ablai Khan avenue.

9

Opera, ballet and classical music

Other cities

Shymkent This is the largest city in south Kazakhstan and is now actually Kazakhstan's third city with 650,000 inhabitants. With a vibrant nightlife and a busy market, it feels like, looks like and is, in fact, very much a Central Asian city, more akin to Uzbekistan just a few kilometres away over the border, than it is to the rest of Kazakhstan. Over 70% of the city population is reckoned to be Kazakh or Uzbek and only 15% Russian. Being much more Kazakh than Russian certainly gives Shymkent a less disciplined feel about it, and this has its good sides to it and its bad sides. It has a renowned and very busy and colourful bazaar which attracts customers and sellers from all over the region, although it still tends to get flooded out with cheap consumer goods from nearby China. But the dazzling fruit stalls laden down with figs, pomegranates, melons, raisins and nuts of every kind, and tended by wizened and weather-beaten Uzbek crones are at least worth a picture or two. It hardly needs saying that you should watch your wallet. Despite its proximity to and affinity with the rest of Central Asia, Shymkent was not untouched by the Soviet mania for industrialisation. It got a particular nasty lead-processing plant in the process, and this has been joined by Shymkent Refinery which processes oil and gas for Kazakhstan and Russia.

One of the best times to visit Shymkent is at Nowruz which is the Iranian New Year around the spring equinox on 21 March 21. This is widely celebrated in Iran, Afghanistan and much of Central Asia. In Shymkent it is celebrated with parties and fireworks and a public holiday. In South Kazakhstan spring comes earlier than in the rest of Kazakhstan which is still often snowbound at the end of March whilst Shymkent is enjoying flowering trees and fresh fruits and vegetables.

Shymkent is also within striking distance, and a day's visit, of some of Kazakhstan's most important tourist sites, i.e. the stunning twelfth century Mausoleum of Khoja Ahmed Yasawi in Turkestan (190 kms to the north-west) which rivals anything in Samarkand and Bukhara, the Aksu Zhabagly Nature Reserve (90 kms to the north-east) which rises to over 4,500 metres and is one of the most biologically diverse areas in Central Asia, and Otrar (100 kms to the north), the ruins of Kazakhstan's finest medieval city, laid waste by the Mongols in the thirteenth century. The train trip from Shymkent to Turkestan takes four hours, but a rented car will get you there in half the time.

Taraz and **Kyzylorda** are the two other cities in the south, and although they are predominantly Kazakh, they have nothing in particular to recommend them. Both have about a quarter of a million people. Taraz lies about 560 kilometres west of Almaty, and 200 kilometres east of Shymkent. Kyzlorda lies about 470 kilometres north-west of Shymkent. Both cities have a venerable history, Taraz claiming to be over two thousand years old, but there is almost no evidence whatsoever of an interesting past. The Soviet blight has put paid to that. However, about

9

20 kilometres to the east of Taraz is the romantic twelfth- century Mausoleum of Aisha Bibi which is said to have inspired Shah Jehan to build the Taj Mahal in India. Kyzylorda, situated on the flood plains of the Syr Darya River, had a brief moment of glory as the national capital in the 1920s, but there is little to see there now. It serves as a local centre for the Kumkol oil fields lying two or three hours to the north in the desert.

Atyrau and **Aktau** and **Uralsk** Of course the most that some (less fortunate) business visitors will see of Kazakhstan are Atyrau and maybe Aktau on the Caspian Sea. These are the oil hubs of Kazakhstan and now you can get direct flights to Atyrau from Amsterdam, Istanbul and Moscow without having to go anywhere near the rest of the country. Atyrau was known until 1992 as Guriyev (after the Russian trader who established it in the seventeenth century). It is situated strategically 10 kms from the mouth of where the Ural River flows into the Caspian Sea. Atyrau was initially founded because of fishing, and in particular for the magnificent sturgeon (and caviare) which are still found in the area. Sturgeon still spawn and breed on the flood plain and the delta of the Ural River, but have been ruthlessly overfished so that the entire caviare industry is in danger of disappearing. However, fishing was supplanted by the oil industry in the twentieth century as Atyrau is the closest town to the onshore Tengiz and offshore Kashagan oilfields. With its 150,000 people it serves as an extraction centre, transhipment point and refinery for the Embla oilfields which have now been in operation for almost one hundred years. Many of the picturesque old Russian buildings are being demolished (as is happening elsewhere in Kazakhstan) to make way for refining facilities, industry and hotels, so that there is not a lot to see in Atyrau apart from the wide, muddy meandering Ural River which divides the town in two. There is no shortage of hotels in town, but the good ones are not cheap (US$300 and upwards a night) and the cheap ones are not good. Many of the expatriates in Atyrau live in mobile home camps outside the city. One expatriate blogger describes the climate in Atyrau as: '*In the winter it is wet cold and horrible (-25°C) and the summer is hot dry and horrible +35°C).*'

9

Aktau is not Kazakhstan's most attractive city, being a new port city built in 1961 on an arid part of the Caspian shore. Like Atyrau it is developing fairly fast because of the expanding offshore oil industry. There are tentative plans to develop a tourist industry, but Aktau is a long way from anywhere and its extreme climate (January average - 4°C and July average + 26°C) limits its attractions. This and stiff winds and dust storms off the desert. But the Caspian beaches do attract tourists from the rest of the country. As in Atyrau, hotel prices are stiff, maybe because of the costs of operating in a remote location, and the fact that busy oil people can probably afford them.

About 600 kilometres north of Atyrau and tucked away in the north-west corner of Kazakhstan, Uralsk (or Oral in Kazakh), feels much more like a central Russian city than anything else. It has managed to retain much of its charming nineteenth-century Russian architecture, including a lovely yellow and white Town Hall as well as a splendid onion-domed Cathedral of Archangel Mikhail from 1750. Uralsk feels less like a Soviet colonial city than most of the other towns in Kazakhstan. Like Atyrau it is built on both sides of the Ural River. It has become prosperous because of the proximity (150 kilometres to the east) of the huge Karachaganak gas and condensate fields being developed by British Gas. It also serves as a service centre for the enormous agricultural areas surrounding this city of 200,000 people.

At the other end of the country in East Kazakhstan close to the borders with Siberian Russia and China are **Semipalatinsk** and **Ust-Kamenogorsk**. These are the Russian names for the Kazakh Semey and Oskemen. Semipalatinsk is known for two things. It was the centre for the Soviet atmospheric (and underground) testing of nuclear weapons for 40 years from 1949, and it was where Fyodor Dostoevsky, the great Russian novelist, spent five years as an exile in the Russian Army. Recovering from its legacy of nuclear testing has not been easy for Semipalatinsk, and horror stories of cases of cancer, leukaemia and deformed unfortunates continue to emerge. The test site is about 150 kilometres west of Semipalatinsk and is known as the 'Polygon'. Should you wish to, it is possible to visit the area and to get to the former closed city of Kurchatov, either by train or bus or by a special trip organised by local travel agents in Semipalatinsk. Otherwise Semipalatinsk is an undistinguished town, but the Dostoevsky Literary Museum housed in the wooden cottage Dostoevsky lived in in the 1850s is certainly worth visiting, as it gives an insight into the great novelist's thought patterns. It is not difficult to see how his great novels arose from his lengthy exile here.

Like many other Kazakh cities Ust-Kamenogorsk started life as a Russian fort in the early eighteenth century, built strategically on the confluence of the Ulba and Irtysh rivers. There are still a few attractive buildings left including a pretty old town, but during Soviet times the city became one of Kazakhstan's most important mineral and metallurgical centres, linked to some extent with the nuclear sites about 500 kilometres to the west. Uranium and beryllium were major products, and the city is still predominantly industrial. However, because of its relative proximity to the Altai Mountains, Ust-Kamenogorsk is a good base for exploring this magnificent area. The Altai Mountains are in fact an enormous mountain chain extending over Russia, China, Mongolia and Kazakhstan, and Kazakhstan only contains the western fringes of the mountain chain. They rise to over 4,000 metres and are some of the remotest, least visited mountains in the world. As such they are still home to many endemic plants and animals. The Scythians who were the first to domesticate the horse and who produced much of the magnificent gold ornaments seen in Kazakhstan's museums, are said to have their origins in the Altai Mountains. Ust-Kamenogorsk is the nearest city to the mountains, but these still lie between 200 and 500 kilometres east and north of the city, so that you have to organise your trip from the city with one of the many local travel agents.

Karaganda which is situated about 200 kilometres south of Astana on the road to Almaty, lies at the centre of a huge, flat industrial plain of coal and iron mines, stretching as far as the eye can see. Karaganda Oblast (or administrative region) of which Karaganda City is the centre is one and a half times the size of the United Kingdom and contains just one and a half million

9

people. This gives an idea of the scale of the country. There is no shortage of air pollution, but, with the sheer size and scale of the steppe, it is quickly lost in the atmosphere. Karaganda was, therefore, one of the Soviet Union's biggest iron and steel producers, and at Temirtau, about 40 kilometres north of Karaganda City is the huge Ispat-Karmet plant, one of the biggest steel producers in the world. To the west of Karaganda is an endless succession of extremely depressing coal mining towns, putting one in mind of the Britain of the 1950s.

Karaganda City is now a pleasant enough, but not very interesting, centre of about 500,000 people, but it has a darker history. Stalin established some eleven Gulag Camps just to the west of the city in the 1930s and over 700,000 people served in them. These were part of Solzhenitsyn's 'Gulag Archipelago' Many of these deported here were Germans and there is still a strong German influence in the city. The forced labour of the inmates was, of course, the basis for Karaganda's industrialisation. Solzhenitsyn's theory, of course, was that the Gulag was a very necessary institution in Stalin's Soviet Union. The very threat of being sent to the Gulag, was sufficient to focus people's minds, to keep their noses to the grindstone and to make sure that industrial targets were met. Fortunately there is not much left to see of the camps themselves although there is a small museum at Dolinka 50 kilometres west of Karaganda City.

Pavlodar, Petropavlovsk and **Kostanay** in the north of Kazakhstan, close to the border with Siberian Russia, are provincial cities with limited national significance, and very similar to their provincial counterparts like Omsk Novosibirsk and Chelyabinsk across the border. All have a history of being Russian outposts or forts from the early eighteenth century in the Russian push to the East, but most of the interesting architecture from that period has been obliterated, and has mainly been consigned to regional museums.

Pavlodar was designated as the capital of the 'Virgin Lands' agricultural programme in the 1950s and, since then, has managed to accumulate large chemical, aluminium and tractor factories. It also serves as a market centre for the huge agricultural collectives surrounding the city. Apart from a few Tsarist houses, Pavlodar is a standard Soviet-issue industrial town, although it has been livened up by a new surrealist Maschur Zhusup Mosque, designed by the Kazakh architect Tolegen Abilda who was also responsible for the futuristic circus building in Astana. With room for a congregation of 1,500 it is difficult to see how it is going to be filled in such a secular part of northern Kazakhstan.

Petropavlovsk, being close to the Russian border, is dominated by ethnic Russians and there is a lot of exchange with Omsk across the border as neither nation requires a visa of the other. Apart from a few nineteenth century residential buildings and the restored residence of Ablai Khan, one of the most important leaders of the Kazakh nation in the second half of the eighteenth century, there is not a lot to see. As has happened in so many Kazakh towns, much has been sacrificed to the needs of new Soviet industry, in this case production of military equipment and machine-building.

9

Kostanay, about 700 kilometres north-west of Astana, is also very close to the Russian border and has many links with Chelyabinsk and other Siberian cities across the border. In fact the border with Russia is hardly noticeable for local residents. Like Pavlodar, Kostanay was a centre for the Virgin Lands, and serves as an agricultural market for the endless prairies outside the city. Again, the needs of Soviet industrialisation and the need to mine Kazakhstan's mineral resources have tended to submerge the city in Soviet administrative architecture. Some of the biggest iron mines in the former Soviet Union are located to the south-west of Kostanay at Rudni and Lisakovsk. There is still a large German community in Kostanai and the surrounding towns, and there are still regular scheduled flights every week from Kostanay to Cologne and Hannover.

10

leisure & tourism

leisure & tourism

Things to do and see in some
cities within Kazakhstan

The business visitor's perennial quandary is what to do on his or her day off? It is not that he or she is not interested in the country's culture or people. There may be lots of fascinating things to see and do. It is simply that businessfolk are there to work, to do the job as quickly and cost-effectively as possible and then to hightail out of there as fast as possible, not costing the firm any more than necessary, and making sure they get back home in time for a child's birthday.

But all of us who have travelled a bit know the sinking feeling when, as soon as you arrive, it is suddenly announced that a two-day official holiday will start the day after tomorrow, and all government offices, businesses and shops will be closed. Hopefully your hotel will still be up to serving breakfast but . . . Your local hosts are delighted at the prospect of two full days with the family whilst you are staring at the prospect of 48 hours of unmitigated boredom.

And we all know that there is little more soul-destroying than being stuck in a strange city, knowing nobody, and with nothing to do! Your host sees you back to your hotel in the evening and says '*Have a nice public holiday*', not realising that the last thing you came to his country for was a day or two off. Of course you can catch up on your notes. But if you have arrived in the country champing at the bit to get on with meetings, and you have not even made any notes to catch up on, it can be difficult to know what to do to pass the time.

10

Of course if you know folk in the country, or if your host decides to take you in hand then you can have a great time. If you are lucky enough to be out in the steppes on one of Kazakhstan's national holidays in summer, and you know some local Kazakhs then you might be invited to join in on a great family party held in a yurt out on the steppe where the food and drink flow freely. Folk play football, throw frisbees, sing traditional songs or simply wander off into the great expanses of rolling grasslands to commune with nature. That is a magnificent way to spend a day off in Kazakhstan, but not one that the casual visitor to the country is likely to experience, unless he is very fortunate.

So normally you are thrown back on your own devices. Sitting working a hotel bedroom whilst everyone else is out enjoying themselves, has limited appeal. So what to do?

As readers will have gathered, Kazakhstan is a huge country. It is therefore not often a question of taking a day trip on the bus to a local tourist site or attraction. Perhaps the most interesting tourist site in Kazakhstan is the magnificent tiled twelfth-century Mausoleum of Khoja Ahmed Yasawi in Turkestan. How about a day **Day trips** trip there? The problem here is that Turkestan is well over 900 kilometres by bus or by train from Almaty (and twice as far from Astana!). To get there on the train from Almaty is an 18 hour trip and you would leave at 6 a.m. and would be in Turkestan just after midnight! And Turkestan's nearest airport is at least a couple of hundred kilometres away. So in Kazakhstan it does not do to be too ambitious on your day off. You stick to the city where you are working. However, in fact there is quite a lot to do in the main Kazakhstan cities on a day off if you use a bit of ingenuity. In Kazakh in our experience leisure time can be divided broadly into three categories, that is: Sports (active and spectator), Nature (the mountains, the steppes, the lakes and birdwatching) and Culture.

10

Sports – for the active

More and more businesspeople realise the need to keep in trim even on a short business trip. The sedentary life with hotel meals and drinks can quickly take its toll, if you don't keep your heart and your lungs in trim. Hence the growing popularity of hotel fitness centres and any hotel worth its hire will have one. But putting in the miles on a treadmill can be a pretty lonesome business and of limited attraction. Lots of businessmen go jogging and the better hotels can often recommend a route and even give you a map.

Anyone who has been on the international business circuit for any length of time will know of the Hash House Harriers (HHH). There are almost 2,000 Hash House Harrier clubs in 183 countries (http://www.gthhh.com). They are usually organised by an informal group of local expatriates who organise what is called a 'fun run' which means a run or a walk of up to five kilometres, following a trail, from a pre-set starting point. They take place every week or fortnight, usually after work, say 6 p.m. The finishing point is usually a pub or a bar where one socialises and meets with other runners to share experiences and get to know the place. It is often an invaluable way for visiting businesspeople to meet the local expatriate community and many nationals who are members as well. Fitness is not a prerequisite. In Kazakhstan it has been described as a 'drinking club with a running problem'. Children and non-drinkers are also welcome. In Almaty the Tian Shan Hash House Harriers ran regularly until 2005, but there seems to have been difficulties in getting runs organised after that. In 2009 there seemed to be none operating on a regular basis, but this may have changed by the time this book reaches the bookshelves. If you are keen to find out if HHH is operating in Almaty or Astana you should check with the embassies or Mad Murphy's bar in Almaty. Someone, somewhere, is at least keeping the home page running at http://www.almatyhhh.com, so you should also keep checking if it has started up again.

hash House Harriers

Otherwise the opportunities for a visiting businessman to keep in trim in Kazakhstan are limited. However, in Almaty the proximity of the Tian Shan Mountains does offer great potential. Winter or summer, an afternoon trip from Almaty at 824 metres altitude, up to Shimbulak which lies 2,200 metres above sea level (nearly 7,000 feet) is certainly worth the trouble. It takes less than half an hour to get to Shimbulak. You can get a service bus, although it is probably more convenient to hire a taxi for the afternoon (costing you say US$50) to take you first to the Medeo High Altitude speed skating rink (known to all skating enthusiasts all over the world) and then on to Shimbulak Ski resort. In winter you can hire skis or a snowboard and join in the fun, or you can simply get yourself a drink and take in the 'après-ski' ambience on a sunny outdoor terrace. You can depend on good snow from the end of October to the end of March. Chairlifts will take you up to almost 3,000 metres. In summer you can walk in the magnificent Tian Shan spruce forests which surround the ski slopes, and, depending on your time and fitness, you can hike on as far as you like. Eventually you will come, after some days, to the border with Kyrgyzstan. The slopes at

10

Skiing

Shimbulak will host the VII Asian Winter Games in 2011 and Kazakhstan expects to spend as much as US$1 billion on new sporting facilities for the Games, including the extensive upgrading of the Medeo Skating Rink. It has been predicted that Shimbulak will become one of the ten greatest ski resorts in the world by 2015. Cross-country skiing is also possible in the winter months in Astana, Karaganda and several other towns in northern Kazakhstan where you can hire cross-country skis. If, in addition to being a smart businessman, you are also very fit and an accomplished skier you can go heli-skiing in the Tian Shan Mountains in summer at altitudes above 4,500 metres. Kan Tengri Expeditions of 10 Kastayev Street, Almaty (http://www.kantengri.kz) offer six days high altitude summer skiing on the borders of Kazakhstan, Kyrgyzstan and China – but whether you can get that sort of trip on the firm is up to you! Kan Tengri (and other Almaty-based firms too) are beginning to offer trekking, mountain biking and horse riding in the Tian Shan, but whether these come within the category of your day off is another matter.

10

Golf

For more leisurely, and more businesslike, sporting activities, Almaty has two good 18 hole golf courses at the Nurtau Golf Club and the Zhailjau Golf Resort, both of them above the city, with a wonderful backdrop of the Tian Shan Mountains. Nurtau, which is over 7,000 yards, is hosting the 5th Kazakhstan Open in September 2009. President Nazarbayev is a keen golfer who encouraged the development of the Nurtau course. Your hotel will be able to arrange a round for you. For tennis, some of the bigger hotels have private courts which you can use if you are a resident.

Bathhouses

It is difficult to know whether to classify the Arasan bathhouse in central Almaty as a sport or part of the culture, but it is certainly an experience not to be missed. They offer Turkish baths, a Russian banya or a Finnish sauna. You sign on for a two-hour session and men and women are of course segregated. A session will cost about 700 *tenge* and rigorous massage is also offered. The baths are open every day of the week from 8 a.m. to 10 p.m. It is a great way to be reinvigorated after a week of business negotiations.

Watching sport –
some suggestions

Watching sport in a foreign country often gives the visitor interesting insights, simply by observing spectator behaviour. The two main spectator sports in Kazakhstan are football (mainly in the summer) and ice hockey (mainly in the winter).

Like other oil-rich nations, Kazakhstan sees the sponsoring of sport, i.e. cycling, football, golf and ice hockey as a way of gaining international prominence. A lot of sponsor money has gone into football, especially into the capital's team FC Lokomotiv Astana. This was formed by an amalgamation of teams (from Almaty and Astana) in February 2009. There are 14 teams (from all over the huge country) in Kazakhstan's Premier League which is played from March to September. The best team in the past couple of seasons has been FK Aktobe, but they were knocked out of the first qualifying round of the UEFA Champion's League in the 2008-2009 season. As FC Lokomotiv Astana play at home every second week (usually on a Saturday or a Sunday) at the brand new stadium due to open in mid 2009 in Astana, it is well worth checking with your hotel reception if they can find out if there is a home game coming up. You can usually buy a ticket at the ground, but it might be an idea to get the hotel to fix a ticket in advance. You can usually expect to be accompanied by about ten thousand spectators which is the average for a home game. On the international football scene Kazakhstan is struggling and is not likely to qualify for the FIFA World Cup Finals 2010 in South Africa.

Football

10

Because of its extreme continental climate, Kazakhstan has always been in the top drawer in ice hockey. The Soviet Union team often drew on Kazakh players. Nowadays the Kontinental Hockey League (KHL) was established in 2008 to rival the US's National Hockey League (NHL). The KHL consists of 24 teams from Russia, Blas, Kazakhstan and Latvia organised in four divisions. Barys ('Snow Leopards') of Astana is the only Kazakh team in the competition. Barys, of course, has to travel all over Russia to play its away games but it plays at home at least every three weeks (often three games in

Ice hockey

that week) at the Alatau Sports Palace in Astana. The season usually runs from early September to the end of February. As Almaty and Astana will host the VII Asian Winter Games in 2011, Astana is building a new ice-hockey stadium to house 15,000 spectators. Professional ice hockey played at this level is extremely fast and exciting and is wonderful for whiling away a couple of hours on an otherwise dull Sunday night. Barys depends heavily on sponsorship and it needs it, as it has contracted top professionals from Canada, Slovakia, the Czech Republic and Russia as well as Kazakhstan itself.

Nature

By nature we mean what you can do, by and large, in the great outdoors. There is something of a paradox in Kazakhstan. Limited areas of the country, especially its cities and industrial areas, are highly polluted, with watercourses laden with industrial waste, and areas out of bounds because of radioactive waste. On the other hand, because it is so huge and has so few people, Kazakhstan also harbours some of the least disturbed natural habitats on the planet. It is not so difficult to avoid the pollution, but it is often difficult to find the natural habitats.

But let us be practical. We are talking about what you do in your day off and not a major expedition. However, even from the two main cities of Almaty and Astana you can experience the vast mountain chains of Central Asia and the timeless steppe landscape of wild horses and wolf packs – and still be back in the hotel in time for dinner. In Almaty itself there are several day trips which will get you far out of the city, and into the 'real' Kazakhstan. Here are some of them:

Charyn-canyon

Charyn Canyon. This is situated about 200 kilometres north-east of Almaty on the way to the border with China. It is a three to four hour drive from the city. Charyn is an 80 kilometre long canyon (up to 300 metres deep), not unlike the Grand Canyon. It is carved by wind and water out of red sandstone. A day trip will cost anything between US$100 and US$200 depending on whether you are sharing a car or not. There is no shortage of travel agents in Almaty who can fix a trip for you. A highlight of the trip is the Valley of the Castles which is a series of fantastically shaped mountains. Some of the trips also take in a vist to the Nura Eagle Hunting Museum on the way home. Here you can meet some of the 50 remaining traditional '*berkutchi*' who use trained golden eagles to hunt small animals (marmots, hares and rabbits) and birds on the open steppe in winter. This traditional sport is said to have been suppressed during the Soviet period, but it is said that Genghis Khan kept over one thousand trained eagles for hunting purposes.

Another day trip which will take you far from the hustle and bustle of the city and out into the wilds is to the Bolshoi Almaty Lake. This is a lake about 30 kilometres south of Almaty, fed by the glaciers of the Tian Shan Mountains and surrounded on three sides by 4,000-metre peaks, and with magnificent alpine air. You can walk from here up the hill through the mountains to the Astronomical Observatory and to a Cosmic Rays Research Laboratory, situated here at 3,300 metres in Soviet times because of the clear air.

Bolshoi Almaty Lake

10

There are several other possible day trips from Almaty itself and there are several travel companies that can help you to organise them. Here are three:

ACS Travel Agency,
Samal 2/63, Almaty 050059
Tel: +7 7272 629037
Email: office@acs-almaty.com

Jibek Joly Travel Agency
Hotel Zhetysu, 55 Ablai Khan Avenue, Almaty 050004
Tel: +7 7272 500407
Email: info@jibekjoly.kz

Advantour Kazakhstan
Oxiana TOO, 28/A Begalin Street, Almaty 050010
Tel: +7 7273 177927
Email: almaty@advantour.com

Travel agents

One other nature site worth visiting in Almaty itself is the Koktobe Mountain on the south side of the city. It rises about 300 metres above the rest of the city and is

Koktobe Mountains

approached by a cable car which starts its one-mile journey on Dostyk Avenue. Apart from the obligatory restaurants and kiosks, one gets a magnificent view into the foothills and the sprawling villages of the Tian Shan Mountains rising impressively to the south.

Sary Arka

Astana, planted firmly in the middle of the great steppe, cannot offer the excursions to areas of great natural beauty which Almaty can. In fact much of the steppe to the north and west of Astana was converted to agricultural land fifty years ago, with endless fields for growing cereals. In the south and west of Astana you soon come upon the Sary Arka or Yellow Back (referring to the yellow feather grass) which is the name given to the great grassy steppelands of Central Kazakhstan, which seem to stretch interminably to the horizon and beyond. These were great, well-watered stretches of waving feather grass, ideal for traditional nomadic horse and animal husbandry.

10

UNESCO World Heritage site

The most accessible part of the Sary Arka from Astana, at least for a day off, is the Tengiz and Korgalzhin Lakes. These are in the Korgalzhin National Park which is about 135 kilometres south-west of Astana, on a not too bad road. You can get to the park in just over two hours. The National Park is part of the UNESCO World Heritage Site: Sary Arka Steppe and Lakes of Northern Kazakhstan (which was inscribed in 2008). It is therefore one of Central Asia's most important natural sites and certainly worth your time if you have a spare day in Astana. It consists of salt lakes and wetlands and undisturbed steppe grasslands and is home to many species of rare and endangered birds such as the Siberian white crane, the Dalmatian pelican and the sociable lapwing. In addition it provides a refuge for the highly endangered Saiga antelope. UNESCO estimates that the area provides feeding for 15 million migratory birds. If you are lucky you will also see the world's most northerly colony of greater flamingoes who migrate from the Caspian to the Tengiz Lake from April to September. This is a relatively remote area with few accommodation or eating facilities so it is probably best to confine your visit to a one-day trip from Astana, unless you are a fanatical birdwatcher who appear to be able to put up with any privation to see their favourite species. It is not difficult to find a travel agency in Astana who can fix a day's trip with a driver for about US$100. It hardly needs saying this trip can only be undertaken from the late spring, say the end of April, to the early Autumn, say mid September.

Also within reach of a day's trip from Astana is Lake Borovoye which is about 250 kilometres north of the capital on the main road north to Kokshetau. This is the centre of the Burabay National Nature Park and is an area of mountains, lakes and picturesque pine forests with walking trails and forest drives. The mountains or hills rise from 200 to 300 metres above the surrounding plains. The area is, of course, in great contrast to much of the rest of northern Kazakhstan and so attracts large numbers of domestic tourists. It is a natural that Borovoye will become a weekend excursion from Astana. Hotels and restaurants are expanding quickly and foreign investors have unveiled huge plans to expand facilities at Borovoye, including Kazakhstan's only casino. In winter there are facilities for downhill and cross-country skiing. It is possible to get to Borovoye by bus from Astana, although the four-hour trip is not particularly alluring. It would be more expensive but more comfortable to hire a car and driver from a local travel agency in Astana who can organise meals (and if necessary accommodation) for a brief trip.

Burabay National Nature Park

10

Of course the above is just a small proportion of the natural sites you can visit within Kazakhstan. As we have said before, the main difficulty in finding day trips in Kazakhstan is the great distances. Although both Almaty and Astana do have possibilities to have a good day out in the country, the opportunities in smaller cities are fewer.

Culture: improving the mind

Although sport or seeing the sights can be a good way of unwinding, a day off can also be used to improve the mind! A day off can give you a chance to learn something new about the country you are in, and to learn something new about an exotic and little-known culture like Kazakhstan's.

As we pointed out in earlier there are many opportunities to see live opera, ballet and classical music in both Almaty and Astana at several venues. The trickiest thing about them is to find when and where they are on, and here it is maybe best to recruit your hotel receptionist's help. Events are always advertised in the Kazakh and Russian press, so it is possible to find out what there is to see. Kazakhstan has three troupes which offer Western classical music, i.e. the State Opera, the State Philharmonic Orchestra and the State Chamber Orchestra. However, Kazakhstan also has its own classical music orchestra which plays Kazakh music on Kazakh instruments. This is the Kazakh State Kurmangazy Orchestra of Folk Instruments which is a full orchestra of up to 100 musicians who play on Western instruments and traditional Kazakh instruments like the *dombra*, the *khobyz* and the Kazakh harp. The fact that the musicians are clad in their highly ornate traditional Kazakh dress makes them one of the most spectacular sights in the world music scene. In 2005 they took the Carnegie Hall by storm so they are certainly worth seeking out, even if the music seems unfamiliar.

10

Museums

But if you have a spare afternoon, and do not want to go home without knowing at least something about Kazakhstan's truly astonishing traditional culture then you have to go to one of two museums. Either the Museum of the President's Cultural Centre on Respublika Avenue in Astana or the Central State Museum on Furmanov Street in Almaty. Both museums show examples of the magnificent Scythian gold and silver jewellery produced by the steppe and mountain cultures of Kazakhstan between the seventh and third centuries BC, and which heavily influenced classical Greek culture which was also emerging at that time. The Astana Museum has a stunning replica/reconstruction of the 'Golden Man' of Issyk kurgan. This is a unique costume and headdress made up of 4,000 pieces of gold, many of them finely worked. This was found at Esik, 40 kilometres east of Almaty, in 1969 and is perhaps the most striking example of Saka/Scythian gold in existence. The original pieces, which are too fragile for display, are said to be kept in the vaults of the Central Bank, but several replicas have been made. Otherwise both museums have good reconstructions of traditional

Kazakh life on the steppe based on the yurt and the herding of camels and horses. A lifestyle which is very fast disappearing. The Central State Museum in Almaty also has a series of souvenir/carpet shops where you can find traditional Kazakh and Turkmen carpets and kelims.

10

appendix one

A1

appendix one

Useful contact addresses

Kazakhstan's Ministry of Foreign Affairs now lists no fewer than 76 Kazakhstan diplomatic missions overseas. The full list is available at: http://portal.mfa.kz/portal/page/portal/mfa/en/content/ministry/missions

The main ones are listed below:

The Main Kazakhstan Embassies

United Kingdom (London)
33 Thurloe Square
London SW7 2SD
United Kingdom
Tel: +44 (0) 20 7581 4646
Tel: +44 (0) 20 7590 3480
Fax: +44 (0) 20 7584 8481
Email: london@kazakhstanembassy.org.uk
Website: http://www.kazakhsstanembassy.org.uk

United States of America (Washington DC)
1401 16th Street N.W.,
Washington DC 20036
Tel: +1 202 232 5488,
Tel: +1 202 550 9617
Fax: +1 202 232 5845
Email: washington@kazakhembus.com
Website: http://www.kazakhembus.com

United States of America (New York: United Nations)
305 E 47th Street, 3rd Floor, New York NY 10017
Tel: +1 212 230 1900
Tel: +1 212 230 1192
Fax: +1 212 230 1172
Email: kazakhstan@un.int
Website: http://www.kazakhstanun.org AND
          http://www.kazconsulny.org

Belgium (Brussels)
Avenue Van Bever, 30, 1180 Bruxelles
Tel: +32 (0) 2 374 95 62
Fax: +32 (0) 2 374 50 91
Email: kazakstan.embassy@swing.be
Website: http://kazakhstanembassy.be

A1

A1

Canada (Ottawa)
283 McLeod Street, Ottawa
Ontario K2P 1A1
Tel: +1 613 788 3704
Fax: +1 613 788 3702
Email: kazconscan@on.aibn.com
Website: http://www.kazconsul.ca

China (Beijing)
9 Dong Liu Jie, San Li Tun
Beijing 100600
Tel: +86 (0) 10 65322550
Tel: +86 (0) 10 65327725
Fax: +86 (0) 10 65326183
Email: kz@kazembchina.org
Website: http://www.kazembchina.org

France (Paris)
59, rue Pierre Charron, 75008 Paris, France
Tel: +33 (0) 1 45615206
Tel: +33 (0) 1 45615200
Fax: +33 (0) 1 45615201
Email: vk001@dial.oleane.com
Website: http://www.amb-kazakhstan.fr

Germany (Berlin)
Bundesrepublik Deutchland Nordendstrasse 14-17, D-
13156 Berlin
Tel: +49 (0) 30 47007111
Tel: +49 (0) 30 47007160
Fax: +49 (0) 30 47007125
Email: info@botschaft-kz.de AND kasqer@ndh.net
Website: http://www.botschaft-kaz.de

Israel (Tel Aviv)
52a, Hayarkon Str., Tel Aviv 63432
Tel: +972 (0) 3 5163411
Tel: +972 (0) 3 5163464
Tel: +972 (0) 3 5163619
Fax: +972 (0) 3 5163437
Email: kzisrael@netvision.net.il
Website: http://www.kazakhemb.org.il

Italy (Rome)
Via Cassia, 471
00189 Roma
Tel: +39 (0) 63 6301130

Tel: +39 (0) 63 6308476
Fax: +39 (0) 63 6292675 and 63 6292612
Email: kazakstan.emb@agora.it
Website: http://www.embkaz.it

Japan (Tokyo)
9-8, Himonya 5-chome, Meguro-ku, Tokyo 152-0003
Tel: +81 (0) 3 37915273
Tel: +81 (0) 3 37915275
Fax: +81 (0) 3 37915279
Email: jpdiplomemb@gmail.com

Russia (Moscow)
01000 Moscow, Chistoprudnii bulvar 3a
Tel: +7 495 9271701
Tel: +7 495 6271809
Tel: +7 495 6081570
Fax: +7 495 6082650 and 6081549
Email: moscow@kazembassy.ru
Website: http://www.kazembassy.ru

Spain (Madrid)
C/ Sotillo, 10 Parque Conde de Orgaz
28043 Madrid
Tel: +34 (0) 917 216290
Tel: +34 (0) 917 216294
Fax: +34 (0) 917 219374
Email: embajada@kazesp.org
Website: http://www.kazesp.org

A1

Turkey (Ankara)
066450 Kilik Ali sokaK 6,

Or – An Diplomatik Sitesi Cankaya,
Ankara
Tel: +90 (0) 312 4919100
Tel: +90 (0) 323 4198266
Fax: +90 (0) 312 4904455
Email: kazank@kazakhstan.org.tr AND
           kazankembassy@mail.ru
Website: http://www.kazakhstan-embassy.org.tr

United Arab Emirates (Abu Dhabi)
PO Box 39556 Al Mushrif w-52 villa No. 61b
Abu Dhabi
Tel: +971 (0) 2 4476623
Fax: +971 (0) 2 4476624
Email: kazemb@emirates.net.ae

Important trade points of contact in UK

UK Trade and Investment (UKTI)
Kingsgate House
66-74 Victoria Street
London SW1 6SW
Tel: +44 (0) 20 7215 8000
Email: enquiries@ukti.gsi.gov.uk
Website: http://www.uktradeinvest.gov.uk

Scottish Development International
Atlantic Quay
150 Broomielaw
Glasgow G2 8LU
Tel: +44 (0) 14 1228 2828
Fax: +44 (0) 14 1228 2089
Website: http://www.sdi.co.uk

International Business Wales
Trafalgar House
5 Fitzalan Place
Cardiff/Caerdydd
CF24 0ED
Tel: + 44 (0) 14 4384 5500
Email: ibw@wales.gsi.gov.uk
Website: http://www.ibwales.com

Invest Northern Ireland
Bedford Square
Bedford Street
Belfast BT2 7ES
Tel: +44 (0) 28 9023 9090
Fax: +44 (0) 28 9043 6536
Email: eo@investni.com
Website: http://www.investni.com

A1

Important trade points of contact in Kazakhstan

Most Embassies in Kazakhstan have their own commercial sections (many of them quite small). Some are in Astana and some are in Almaty (and some are split between the two!) and you will have to check with your own Embassy. The following

UK Trade and Invest
The British Embassy
Kosmonatov Street 62
RENC Building 6th Floor
Astana 010000
Tel: +7 7172 556237

UK Trade and Invest (UKTI)
West Kazakhstan Trade Office (Oil & Gas)
Office 2101
Renco Building
55 Aiteke Bi Street
Atyrau 060011
Tel: +7 7122 271748
Fax: +7 7122 271752

US Commercial Service
41 Kazibek bi Street
Almaty 050010
Tel: +7 7272 507612

American Chamber of Commerce
Hyatt Hotel, Office Tower, 10th floor
Almaty 050040
Tel: +7 7272 587938
Fax: +7 7272 587942
Email: info@amcham.kz
Website: http://www.amcham.kz

The European Union Cooperation Office
20A Kazibek bi Street,
Almaty 050010
Tel: +7 7272 980343
Fax: +7 7272 910749
Email: delegation-kazakhstan@ec.europa.eu

KAZINVEST,
67 Aiteke bi Street,
Almaty 480091
Tel: +7 7272 625297
Email: kazinvest@kazinvest.kz
Website: http://www.kazinvest.kz

A1

appendix two

appendix two

Law firms in Kazakhstan

As we have pointed out before in this book, unless you are fluent in Russian and very conversant with post-Soviet bureaucratic procedures it is a smart idea to hire yourself local legal advice if you are going to embark on complex business matters in Kazakhstan. Here is a selection of local firms:

AKTAU
GRATA Law Firm
Apt. 110, building #12, 7 district
Aktau
Tel: +7 729 2531043

AKTOBE
GRATA Law Firm
Office 213, 18, 8 March Street
Aktobe
Tel: +7 713 2221791

ALMATY
Assistance LLC Law Firm
153/50A Zharokov Street
Almaty
Tel: +7 727 2752667

Baker & McKenzie
8th Floor 155 Abai Avenue
Almaty
Tel: +7 727 2509945

Bracewell & Patterson, LLP
65 Kazybek Bi Str. Suite 410
Almaty
Tel: +7 727 2581400

Bracewell and Giuliani,
57 Amangeldy St.
Almaty
Tel: +7 727 2581400

Chadbourne & Parke LLP
43 Dostyk Avenue
Dostyk Business Centre, 4th Floor
Almaty
Tel: +7 727 2585088

A2

Denton Wilde Sapte
38 Dostyk Prospect, Suite 703
Almaty
Tel: +7 7272 917422

Dewey & LeBoeuf, LLP
38 Prospekt Dostyk
Ken Dala Business Centre, 5th Floor
Almaty
Tel: +7 7272 507575

Erbol, Zhanar & Dana
Abai avenue 143, 313 office
Almaty
Tel: +7 7272 422487

Global Tax Solutions LLP
99 Panfilov Str.
Almaty
Tel: +7 7272 373371

GRATA Law Firm
39 Gogol Street,
Almaty
Tel: +7 7272 590112

LeBoeuf, Lamb, Greene & MacRae LLP
Ken Dala Business Centre, 5th Floor
Prospekt Dostyk, 38
Almaty
Tel: +7 7272 507576

Macleod Dixon LLP
3 Floor, 1/1 Dzhandosov St.
Almaty
Tel: +7 7272 509380

McGuireWoods Kazakhstan
20 a Kazibek Bi St.
Almaty
Tel: +7 7272 596100

Michael Wilson and Partners, Ltd
Nurly Tau Business Centre, 7th Floor,
Building 1A 5 Al-Farabi Avenue
Almaty
Tel: +7 7272 584890

A2

Salans Almaty
135 Abylai Khan
Almaty
Tel: +7 7272 582380

Signum Law Firm
1st floor, Building 20
'Samal-2' Microdistrict
Almaty
Tel: +7 7272 954370

Sovremennoe Pravo LLC
Timiryazev Str.71
Almaty
Tel: +7 70172 97672

White & Case LLP
Almaty 64 Amangeldy Street
Tel: +7 7272 507491

ASTANA
Astana Law Partners LLP
Bigeldinov Street 54
Suite 407
Astana
Tel: +7 7172 236148 ext. 143

GRATA Law Firm
33 Zheltoksan Street
Astana
Tel: +7 7172 327807

A2

Magisters Astana
Astana Tower
12 Samal Microdistrict
Astana
Tel: +7 7172 592576

ATYRAU
GRATA Law Firm
4 G. Khakimov Street
Atyrau
Tel: +7 7122 352491

Macleod Dixon LLP
Office 902A, 48 Azattyk Ave.
Atyrau
Tel: +7 7122 586897, +7 3122 586898

appendix three

appendix three

As has been emphasized elsewhere in this guide, it is going to be some time before the visiting businessman can dispense with the services of translators and interpreters in Kazakhstan. In most parts of the world most businessfolk are preoccupied with learning English, and in this Kazakhstan is no exception. The situation in Kazakhstan is complicated, however, by the fact that it already has one lingua franca, i.e. Russian, which is understood by 90% of the population, but the government is attempting to introduce a new one, i.e. Kazakh. This situation certainly means that English is making fewer inroads in Kazakhstan than it is elsewhere, e.g. in China. Thus the continued need for translators and interpreters.

One consolation is that, although it costs you money, it is also an excellent way of getting to know the locals and to get a feel for the country. Here is a list:

Almaty
Almaty Translation Centre,
85 a Dostyk Ave. Office 404
Almaty
Tel: +7 7272 664931; +7 7272 664932

Ace Translations Group
65 Furmanov Street
Almaty
Tel: +7 7272 738008; +7 7272 734751

Advanced Translation
144 Chaykovsky Str.
Office 158
Almaty
Tel: +7 7272 616025; +7 7272 720705

AMK Passport Translation
43 Kunayev Str.
Office 205
Almaty
Tel: +7 7272 373418; +7 7272 730471

Business Translation
202 Dostyk Ave.
Business Centre 'Forum'
Almaty
Tel: +7 7272 375076

A3

English Art Centre
59a Turkebayev Str.
Office 22
Almaty
Tel: +7 7272 406216

Expert-Club
272 Bogenbay Batyr Str.
Office 102
Almaty
Tel: +7 7272 779351; + 7272 778534

Excellent English
148 Bogenbay Batyr Str.
Office 410
Almaty
Tel: +7 7272 274056; +7 7272 619588

Alfatiha
55 Abylay Khan ave.
Zhetysu Hotel
Office 127
Almaty
Tel: +7 7272 503560; +7 7272 500400

EPMG
82 Auezov Str.
Office 506
Almaty
Tel: +7 7272 698163

Astana

INTERA LLC
69 Kenesary Str. (Housing Estate "Kaminniy")
Astana
Tel: +7 7172 9710 87/88/89
Website: www.intera.kz
Email: info@intera.kz

ABBA
16 Kenessary Str.
'Zhas-Amir' Business Centre
Astana
Tel: +7 7172 323319

Alem
20 Imanov Str.
Astana
Tel: +7 7172 979942

A3

Atyrau
Centre Lingva
17 Dosmukhambetov Str.
Tel: +7 7122 326022

Western Group
48 Azattyk Ave.
Office 205
Tel: +7 7122 970102
           +7 7122 970079

Poliglot
25 Kurmangazy Str.
Tel: +7 7122 204899

Karaganda
"ABCOM",
33 Bulvar Mira Str.
Tel: +7 7212 42-14-80

SPECTRUM SERVICES ZHV
78 B Baitursynov Str
Tel: +7 7212 920807,
           +7 7212 463442

ABCom
33 Bulvar Mira Str.
Tel: +7 7004 503197
Shymkent

Asyl Asset
43 Tauke Khan Ave.
Tel: +7 7252 550363

Ust-Kamenmogorsk
'TRANSLATOR'
23 Gagarin Str.
Tel: +7 7232 423689

Lotos
Proletarskaya Str.
Tel: +7 7232 241937

Translations Bureau
Tel: +7 7052 185021

A3

appendix four

A4

appendix four

Russian Language

Russian belongs to the East Slavonic group of languages, together with Ukrainian and Belarusian (or Belorussian). It has a reputation for being a difficult language to learn, chiefly due to its use of the Cyrillic alphabet and an extensive case system for nouns and adjectives. The verbs conjugate as well, something which can come as a shock if you were never "lucky" enough to study Latin at school. Also unnerving at first is the absence of definite and indefinite articles ("the" and "a/an" in English), and the almost total lack of the verb "to be" in the present tense. If you want to know where the station is, in Russian the phrase is literally "Where station?".

Pronunciation in Russian should hold few surprises to speakers of either English or most European languages, although the language's range of "hush" sybillants (sh, sch, shch) is wider than most. There is one particular vowel sound, "ы", normally transliterated as a "y", which you will struggle to find in any other language – probably the closest way it can be expressed in words is as a normal short "i"(as in "kitchen"), but pronounce it with your tongue towards the back of your mouth, rather than the front. The Russian alphabet also includes two qualifying symbols, a soft sign "ь" and rarely seen hard sign "ъ" which both affect the pronunciation of the consonant which immediately precedes them. You will not see the hard sign in the samples below, but where there is a soft sign it will be expressed as an apostrophe in line with convention.

Stress is important in Russian, something made more annoying by the fact that it can move about on the same word depending on its form (case, number, person). In the examples below, the stressed syllable is shown in bold. Whether a syllable is stressed or not affects both the sound of the vowel and the meaning of the word, so keep it in mind. Also bear in mind that, in common with some other languages, such as French and German, Russian uses the plural second person "you" form in formal conversation or to convey respect.

If you want to learn Russian properly – by all means go for it. It is a beautiful, melodic and expressive language. Bear in mind, however, that it will require both commitment and time, the latter of which you may not have if you are in business. I suggest that you at least try

A4

to master the alphabet – it looks a bit strange at first, but believe me you will become accustomed to it more quickly that you expect. Above all, try to use at least some of the words and phrases below – Russians are very generous and encouraging with anyone attempting the language, and a few choice phrases will always go down well. Try and remember at all times that Russian is a soft sounding language, whatever may be your preconceptions of it. Keep the consonants gentle and un-aspirated and the rest of it will follow.

The Cyrillic alphabet

Cyrillic is a synthesis of Latin and Greek character-sets, with a few more thrown in to express particular sounds. Apart from Russian, Cyrillic is used in a number of other Slavonic (eg. Ukrainian, Bulgarian, Serbo-Croat) and non-Slavonic (eg. Kazakh, Uzbek, Mongolian) languages. Below is a pronunciation guide – all vowel-sounds are for the vowel in stressed positions. Some of the pronunciation examples may look strange, but they are the closest available to the actual sounds in Russian.

A4

Letter	Transliteration	Pronunciation
а	a	cut
б	b	big
в	v	very
г	g	golf
д	d	dog
е	ye	yet
ё	yo	yonder
ж	zh	montage
з	z	zoo
и	i	sheep
й	y	young
к	k	cable
л	l	love
м	m	mast
н	n	number
о	o	short
п	p	pull

р	r	roll
с	s	small
т	t	tower
у	u	boot
ф	f	foot
х	kh	archive
ц	ts	mints
ч	ch	cheese
ш	sh	shuffle
щ	shch	horse-chestnut
ъ	–	–
ы	y	green (see above)
ь	–	–
э	e	tent
ю	yu	future
я	ya	young

Basics

Yes	Da
No	Nyet
Hello	Zdravstvuytye
Goodbye	Do svidanya
Please	Pozhaluysta
Thank you	Spasibo
Thank you very much	Spasibo bol'shoye

Good morning	Dobroye utro
Good afternoon	Dobry dyen'
Good evening	Dobry vyechyer
Good night	Spokoynoy nochi

Making conversation

My name is Chris	Menya zovut Chris
What is your name?	Kak vas zovut?
Nice to meet you	Ochen' priyatno
How are you?	Kak dela?
Fine, thanks	Normal'no, spasibo
Very well, thanks	Ochen' khorosho, spasibo

A4

Do you speak English?	Vy govoritye po angliyski?
I don't speak Russian	Ya ne govoryu po russki
I speak a little Russian	Ya nemnozhko govoryu po russki
This is my first time in Russia	Eto moy pyervy raz v Rossii
I am from the United Kingdom	Ya iz Vyelikobritanii
I am from the United States	Ya iz Soyedinyonnykh Shtatov
I am from Australia	Ya iz Avstralii
I am from Canada	Ya iz Kanady
I am from Germany	Ya iz Germanii
I am from France	Ya iz Frantsii
Excuse me	Izvinitye
After you	Proshu vas
That's alright	Nye za chto

Numbers

One	Odin
Two	Dva
Three	Tri
Four	Chetyrye
Five	Pyat'
Six	Shest'
Seven	Syem'
Eight	Vosem'
Nine	Dyevyat'
Ten	Dyesyat'
Eleven	Odinnadtsat'
Twelve	Dvyenadtsat'
Thirteen	Trinadtsat'
Fourteen	Chetyrnadtsat'
Fifteen	Pyatnadtsat'
Sixteen	Shestnadtsat'
Seventeen	Syemnadtsat'
Eighteen	Vosyemnadtsat'

A4

Nineteen	Devyatnadtsat'
Twenty	Dvadtsat'
Thirty	Tridtsat'
Forty	Sorok
Fifty	Pyatdyesyat
Sixty	Shest'dyesyat
Seventy	Syem'dyesyat
Eighty	Vosyem'dyesyat
Ninety	Dyevyanosto
Hundred	Sto
Two hundred	Dvyesti
Three hundred	Trista
Four hundred	Chetyresta
Five hundred	Pyat'sot
Six hundred	Shest'sot
Seven hundred	Syem'sot
Eight hundred	Vosyem'sot
Nine hundred	Dyevyat'sot
Thousand	Tysyacha
Million	Million
Billion	Milliard
Once	(Odin) raz
Twice	Dva raza
Five times	Pyat' raz
First	Pyervy
Second	Vtoroy
Third	Tryetiy
Last	Poslyedniy

A4

Questions

Why...?	Pochemu...?
How...?	Kak...?
How much/many...?	Skol'ko...?
Can...?	Mozhno...?

Time

When...?	Kogda...?

Now	Seychas
Then	Togda
Soon	Skoro
Sometime	Kogda-to
Anytime	Kogda-nibud'
Always	Vsegda
Never	Nikogda
Today	Syevodnya
Yesterday	Vchera
Tomorrow	Zavtra
Day	Dyen'
Hour	Chas
Minute	Minuta
Second	Syekunda
What time is it?	Skol'ko vryemyeni?
It is two o'clock	Dva chasa
It is half past two	Poltryet'evo
It is ten to three	Byez desyati tri

Days

What day is it?	Syevodnya kakoy dyen'?
Monday	Ponyedyel'nik
Tuesday	Vtornik
Wednesday	Sryeda
Thursday	Chetvyerg
Friday	Pyatnitsa
Saturday	Subbota
Sunday	Voskryesyen'ye

Place

Where...?	Gdye...?
Here	Zdyes'
There	Tam
Somewhere	Gdye-to
Anywhere	Gdye-nibud'
Everywhere	Vezdye
Nowhere	Nigdye
Near	Blizko
Far	Daleko

A4

(To the) right	(Na-)pravo
(To the) left	(Na-)lyevo
Entrance	Vkhod
Exit	Vykhod

Useful places

Shop	Magazin
Station	Vokzal
Airport	Aeroport
Hotel	Gostinitsa
Museum	Muzyey
Office	Ofis
Restaurant	Restoran
Hospital	Bol'nitsa
Post Office	Pochtamt
Chemist	Aptyeka
Police	Militsiya

Common adjectives

Large	Bol'shoy
Small	Malenkiy
Wide	Shirokiy
Narrow	Uzkiy
Long	Dlinny
Short	Korotkiy
High	Vysokiy
Low	Nizkiy
Fast	Bystry
Slow	Myedlyenny

A4

Instructions

Look	Smotritye
Give me	Daytye
Take this	Voz'mitye
Come here	Iditye syuda
Go away	Ukhoditye
Hurry up	Bystryeye
Stop	Stop

Useful phrases

How much to get to the centre?	Do tsentra skol'ko?
Where is the station?	Gdye vokzal?
Where is the check-in desk?	Gdye registratsiya?
I have a reservation	U menya bron'
Do you have a room?	U vas nomer yest'?
I need the room for two days	Mnye nuzhen nomer na dvye nochi
Do you have a quieter room?	U vas yest' nomer po-tishche?
Where can I change money?	Gdye mozhno dyen'gi pomyenyat'?
Do you have a menu in English?	U vas yest' myenyu na angliyskom?
Can I have the bill?	Mozhno schyot pozhaluysta
Do you have Wi-Fi here?	U vas yest' Wi-Fi zdyes'?
Where can I charge my phone?	Gdye mozhno telefon zaryadit'?

A4